Modern Critical Interpretations

Samuel Beckett's
Waiting for Godot

Modern Critical Interpretations

These and other titles in preparation

Modern Critical Interpretations

Samuel Beckett's
Waiting for Godot

Edited and with an introduction by

Harold Bloom
Sterling Professor of the Humanities
Yale University

Chelsea House Publishers
NEW YORK ◇ **PHILADELPHIA**

© 1987 by Chelsea House Publishers,

a subsidiary of Haights Cross Communications.

Introduction © 1987 by Harold Bloom

Printed and bound in the United States of America

10   9   8   7   6

∞ The paper used in this publication meets the minimum requirements of the American National Standard for Permanence of Paper for Printed Library Materials, Z39.48–1984.

Library of Congress Cataloging-in-Publication Data
Samuel Beckett's Waiting for Godot.
    (Modern critical interpretations)
    Bibliography: p.
    Includes index.
    1. Beckett, Samuel, 1906–   . En attendant
Godot. Bloom, Harold. II. Series.
PQ2603.E378E677   1987   842'.914   86-34301
ISBN 1-55546-058-5

Contents

Editor's Note

This book gathers together a representative selection of the best criticism devoted to Samuel Beckett's tragicomedy *Waiting for Godot*. The critical essays are reprinted here in the chronological order of their original publication. I am grateful to Peter Childers for his work in researching this volume.

My introduction sets the play in the context of Beckett's literary cosmos, Gnostic and Schopenhauerian. John Fletcher begins the chronological sequence of criticism by describing *Godot* as "a meditative rhapsody on the nullity of human attainment," an account consonant with Martin Esslin's investigation of the play as being "essentially *absurd*."

For Ruby Cohn, *Godot* is a vision of waiting that yet can perform "the Nothing." Hugh Kenner, high priest of literary modernism, rejects the notion that the play has a philosophy of life, and associates it instead with the art of Laurel and Hardy.

In Richard Gilman's reading, the play leaves *us* waiting for a story and an ending. Bert O. States relates the language of myth in *Godot* to a crucial paradox of St. Augustine's, phrased by Beckett himself as, "Do not despair; one of the thieves was saved. Do not presume; one of the thieves was damned."

Eric Gans, writing from a deconstructive perspective, sees *Godot* as staging a problematic victory over its own deliberate abstention from that "resentment" that Nietzsche saw as being definitive of modern culture. Tracing affinities between Beckett and Rabelais, Edith Kern returns us to the play's possibilities of tragicomic seriousness, of a kind of religious intensity.

Introduction

Jonathan Swift, so much the strongest ironist in the language as to have no rivals, wrote the prose masterpiece of the language in *A Tale of a Tub*. Samuel Beckett, as much the legitimate descendant of Swift as he is of his friend James Joyce, has written the prose masterpieces of the language in this century, sometimes as translations from his own French originals. Such an assertion does not discount the baroque splendors of *Ulysses* and *Finnegans Wake*, but prefers to them the purity of *Murphy* and *Watt*, and of Beckett's renderings into English of *Malone Dies*, *The Unnamable*, and *How It Is*. Unlike Swift and Joyce, Beckett is only secondarily an ironist and, despite his brilliance at tragicomedy, is something other than a comic writer. His Cartesian dualism seems to me less fundamental than his profoundly Schopenhauerian vision. Perhaps Swift, had he read and tolerated Schopenhauer, might have turned into Beckett.

A remarkable number of the greatest novelists have found Schopenhauer more than congenial: one thinks of Turgenev, Tolstoy, Zola, Hardy, Conrad, Thomas Mann, even of Proust. As those seven novelists have in common only the activity of writing novels, we may suspect that Schopenhauer's really horrifying system helps a novelist to do his work. This is not to discount the intellectual and spiritual persuasiveness of Schopenhauer. A philosopher who so deeply affected Wagner, Nietzsche, Wittgenstein, and (despite his denials) Freud, hardly can be regarded only as a convenient aid to storytellers and storytelling. Nevertheless, Schopenhauer evidently stimulated the arts of fiction, but why? Certain it is that we cannot read *The World as Will and Representation* as a work of fiction. Who could bear it as fiction? Supplementing his book, Schopenhauer characterizes the Will to Live:

Here also life presents itself by no means as a gift for enjoyment, but as a task, a drudgery to be performed; and in accordance with this we see, in great and small, universal need, ceaseless cares, constant pressure, endless strife, compulsory activity, with extreme exertion of all the powers of body and mind. . . . All strive, some planning, others acting; the tumult is indescribable. But the ultimate aim of it all, what is it? To sustain ephemeral and tormented individuals through a short span of time in the most fortunate case with endurable want and comparative freedom from pain, which, however, is at once attended with ennui; then the reproduction of this race and its striving. In this evident disproportion between the trouble and the reward, the will to live appears to us from this point of view, if taken objectively, as a fool, or subjectively, as a delusion, seized by which everything living works with the utmost exertion of its strength for something that is of no value. But when we consider it more closely, we shall find here also that it is rather a blind pressure, a tendency entirely without ground or motive.

Hugh Kenner suggests that Beckett reads Descartes as fiction. Beckett's fiction suggests that Beckett reads Schopenhauer as truth. Descartes as a precursor is safely distant; Joyce was much too close, and *Murphy* and even *Watt* are Joycean books. Doubtless, Beckett turned to French in *Molloy* so as to exorcise Joyce, and certainly, from *Malone Dies* on, the prose when translated back into English has ceased to be Joycean. Joyce is to Beckett as Milton was to Wordsworth. *Finnegans Wake,* like *Paradise Lost,* is a triumph demanding study; Beckett's trilogy, like *The Prelude,* internalizes the triumph by way of the compensatory imagination, in which experience and loss become one. Study does little to unriddle Beckett or Wordsworth. The Old Cumberland Beggar, Michael, Margaret of *The Ruined Cottage;* these resist analysis as do Molloy, Malone, and the Unnamable. Place my namesake, the sublime Poldy, in *Murphy* and he might fit, though he would explode the book. Place him in *Watt?* It cannot be done, and Poldy (or even Earwicker) in the trilogy would be like Milton (or Satan) perambulating about in *The Prelude.*
    The fashion (largely derived from French misreaders of German thought) of denying a fixed, stable ego is a shibboleth of current crit-

icism. But such a denial is precisely like each literary generation's assertion that it truly writes the common language rather than a poetic diction. Both stances define modernism, and modernism is as old as Hellenistic Alexandria. Callimachus is as modernist as Joyce, and Aristarchus, like Hugh Kenner, is an antiquarian modernist or modernist antiquarian. Schopenhauer dismissed the ego as an illusion, life as torment, and the universe as nothing, and he rightly credited these insights to that great modernist, the Buddha. Beckett too is as modernist as the Buddha, or as Schopenhauer, who disputes with Hume the position of the best writer among philosophers since Plato. I laugh sometimes in reading Schopenhauer, but the laughter is defensive. Beckett provokes laughter, as Falstaff does, or in the mode of Shakespeare's clowns.

II

In his early monograph, *Proust*, Beckett cites Schopenhauer's definition of the artistic procedure as "the contemplation of the world independently of the principle of reason." Such more-than-rational contemplation gives Proust those Ruskinian or Paterian privileged moments that are "epiphanies" in Joyce but which Beckett mordantly calls "fetishes" in Proust. Transcendental bursts of radiance necessarily are no part of Beckett's cosmos, which resembles, if anything at all, the Demiurge's creation in ancient Gnosticism. Basilides or Valentinus, Alexandrian heresiarchs, would have recognized instantly the world of the trilogy and of the major plays: *Waiting for Godot, Endgame, Krapp's Last Tape*. It is the world ruled by the Archons, the *kenoma*, non-place of emptiness. Beckett's enigmatic spirituality quests, though sporadically, for a void that is a fulness, the Abyss or *pleroma* that the Gnostics called both forefather and foremother. Call this a natural rather than a revealed Gnosticism in Beckett's case, but Gnosticism it is nevertheless. Schopenhauer's quietism is at last not Beckett's, which is to say that for Beckett, as for Blake and for the Gnostics, the Creation and the Fall were the same event.

The young Beckett, bitterly reviewing a translation of Rilke into English, memorably rejected Rilke's transcendental self-deceptions, where the poet mistook his own tropes as spiritual evidences:

> Such a turmoil of self-deception and naif discontent gains
> nothing in dignity from that prime article of the Rilkean
> faith, which provides for the interchangeability of Rilke

and God. . . . He has the fidgets, a disorder which may very well give rise, as it did with Rilke on occasion, to poetry of a high order. But why call the fidgets God, Ego, Orpheus and the rest?

In 1938, the year that *Murphy* was belatedly published, Beckett declared his double impatience with the language of transcendence and with the transcendence of language, while intimating also the imminence of the swerve away from Joyce in the composition of *Watt* (1942–44):

> At first it can only be a matter of somehow finding a method by which we can represent this mocking attitude towards the word, through words. In this dissonance between the means and their use it will perhaps become possible to feel a whisper of that final music or that silence that underlies All.
>
> With such a program, in my opinion, the latest work of Joyce has nothing whatever to do. There it seems rather to be a matter of an apotheosis of the word. Unless perhaps Ascension to Heaven and Descent to Hell are somehow one and the same.

As a Gnostic imagination, Beckett's way is Descent, in what cannot be called a hope to liberate the sparks imprisoned in words. Hope is alien to Beckett's mature fiction, so that we can say its images are Gnostic but not its program, since it lacks all program. A Gnosticism without potential transcendence is the most negative of all possible negative stances, and doubtless accounts for the sympathetic reader's sense that every crucial work by Beckett necessarily must be his last. Yet the grand paradox is that lessness never ends in Beckett.

III

"Nothing is got for nothing." That is the later version of Emerson's law of Compensation, in the essay "Power" of *The Conduct of Life*. Nothing is got for nothing even in Beckett, this greatest master of nothing. In the progression from *Murphy* through *Watt* and the trilogy onto *How It Is* and the briefer fictions of recent years, there is loss for the reader as well as gain. The same is true of the movement from *Godot, Endgame,* and *Krapp's Last Tape* down to the short plays of Beckett's current and perhaps final phase. A wild humor abandons Beckett, or is transformed into a comedy for which we seem not to be ready. Even an uncommon reader can long for those marvelous Pythagoreans, Wylie and Neary, who are the delight of *Murphy,* or for the sense of the picturesque that makes a last stand in *Molloy.* Though the mode was Joyce's, the music of Wylie and Neary is Beckett's alone:

> "These are dark sayings," said Wylie.
>
> Neary turned his cup upside down.
>
> "Needle," he said, "as it is with the love of the body, so with the friendship of the mind, the full is only reached by admittance to the most retired places. Here are the pudenda of my psyche."
>
> "Cathleen," cried Wylie.
>
> "But betray me," said Neary, "and you go the way of Hippasos."
>
> "The Adkousmatic, I presume," said Wylie. "His retribution slips my mind."
>
> "Drowned in a puddle," said Neary, "for having divulged the incommensurability of side and diagonal."
>
> "So perish all babblers," said Wylie. . . .
>
> "Do not quibble," said Neary harshly. "You saved my life. Now palliate it."
>
> "I greatly fear," said Wylie, "that the syndrome known as life is too diffuse to admit of palliation. For every symptom that is eased, another is made worse. The horse leech's daughter is a closed system. Her quantum of wantum cannot vary."
>
> "Very prettily put," said Neary.

One can be forgiven for missing this, even as one surrenders these easier pleasures for the more difficult pleasures of *How It Is:*

> my life above what I did in my life above a little of everything tried everything then gave up no worse always a hole a ruin always a crust never any good at anything not made for that farrago too complicated crawl about in corners and sleep all I wanted I got it nothing left but go to heaven.

The Sublime mode, according to a great theorist, Angus Fletcher, has "the direct and serious function of destroying the slavery of pleasure." Beckett is certainly the strongest Western author living in the year 1987, the last survivor of the sequence that includes Proust, Kafka, and Joyce. It seems odd to name Beckett, most astonishing of minimalists, as a representative of the Sublime mode, but the isolation and terror of the High Sublime return in the catastrophe creations of Beckett, in that vision Fletcher calls "catastrophe as a gradual grinding down and slowing to a dead stop." A Sublime that moves towards silence necessarily relies upon a rhetoric of waning lyricism, in which the entire scale of effects is transformed, as John Hollander notes:

> Sentences, phrases, images even, are the veritable arias in the plays and the later fiction. The magnificent rising of the kite at the end of *Murphy* occurs in a guarded but positive surge of ceremonial song, to which he will never return.

Kafka's Hunter Gracchus, who had been glad to live and was glad to die, tells us that "I slipped into my winding sheet like a girl into her marriage dress. I lay and waited. Then came the mishap." The mishap, a moment's error on the part of the death-ship's pilot, moves Gracchus from the heroic world of romance to the world of Kafka and of Beckett, where one is neither alive nor dead. It is Beckett's peculiar triumph that he disputes with Kafka the dark eminence of being the Dante of that world. Only Kafka, or Beckett, could have written the sentence in which Gracchus sums up the dreadfulness of his condition: "The thought of helping me is an illness that has to be cured by taking to one's bed." Murphy might have said that; Malone is beyond saying anything so merely expressionistic. The "beyond" is where Beckett's later fictions and plays reside. Call it the silence, or the abyss, or the reality beyond the pleasure principle, or the metaphysical or spiritual reality of our existence at last exposed, beyond further illusion. Beckett cannot or will not name it, but he has worked through to the art of representing it more persuasively than anyone else.

IV

Hugh Kenner wisely observes that, in *Waiting for Godot*, bowler hats "are removed for thinking but replaced for speaking." Such accurate observation is truly Beckettian, even as was Lyndon

Johnson's reflection that Gerald Ford was the one person in Washington who could not walk and chew gum at the same time. Beckett's tramps, like President Ford, keep to one activity at a time. Entropy is all around them and within them, since they inhabit, they are, that cosmological emptiness the Gnostics named as the *kenoma*.

Of the name *Godot*, Beckett remarked, "and besides, there is a rue Godot, a cycling racer named Godot, so you see, the possibilities are rather endless." Actually, Beckett seems to have meant Godet, the director of the Tour de France, but even the mistake is Beckettian, and reminds us of a grand precursor text, Alfred Jarry's "The Passion Considered as an Uphill Bicycle Race," with its superb start: "Barabbas, slated to race, was scratched."

Nobody is scratched in *Waiting for Godot,* but nobody gets started either. I take it that "Godot" is an emblem for "recognition," and I thereby accept Deirdre Bair's tentative suggestion that the play was written while Beckett waited for recognition, for his novels to be received and appreciated, within the canon. A man waiting for recognition is more likely than ever to be obsessed that his feet should hurt continually, and perhaps to be provoked also to the memory that his own father invariably wore a bowler hat and a black coat.

A play that moves from "Nothing to be done" (referring to a recalcitrant boot) on to "Yes, let's go," after which they do not move, charmingly does not progress at all. Time, the enemy above all others for the Gnostics, is the adversary in *Waiting for Godot,* as it was in Beckett's *Proust.* That would be a minor truism, if the play were not set in the world made not by Plato's Demiurge but by the Demiurge of Valentinus, for whom time is hardly the moving image of eternity:

> When the Demiurge further wanted to imitate also the boundless, eternal, infinite, and timeless nature of the Abyss, but could not express its immutable eternity, being as he was a fruit of defect, he embodied their eternity in times, epochs, and great numbers of years, under the delusion that by the quantity of times he could represent their infinity. Thus truth escaped him and he followed the lie.

Blake's way of saying this was to remind us that in equivocal worlds up and down were equivocal. Estragon's way is: "Who am I to tell my private nightmares to if I can't tell them to you?" Lucky's way is the most Gnostic, since how could the *kenoma* be described any better than this?

> the earth in the great cold the great dark the air and the earth abode of stones in the great cold alas alas in the year of their Lord six hundred and something the air the earth the sea the earth abode of stones in the great deeps the great cold on sea on land and in the air I resume for reasons unknown in spite of the tennis the facts are there but time will tell I resume alas alas on on in short in fine on on abode of stones who can doubt it I resume but not so fast I resume the skull fading fading fading and concurrently simultaneously what is more for reasons unknown.

Description that is also lament—that is the only lyricism possible for the Gnostic, ancient or modern, Valentinus or Schopenhauer, Beckett or Shelley:

> Art thou pale for weariness
> Of climbing heaven and gazing on the earth,
>   Wandering companionless
> Among the stars that have a different birth—
> And ever changing, like a joyless eye
> That finds no object worth its constancy?

Shelley's fragment carefully assigns the stars to a different birth, shared with our imaginations, a birth that precedes the Creation–Fall that gave us the cosmos of *Waiting for Godot*. When the moon rises, Estragon contemplates it in a Shelleyan mode: "Pale for weariness . . . of climbing heaven and gazing on the likes of us." This negative epiphany, closing act 1, is answered by another extraordinary Shelleyan allusion, soon after the start of act 2:

> VLADIMIR: We have that excuse.
> ESTRAGON: It's so we won't hear.
> VLADIMIR: We have our reasons.
> ESTRAGON: All the dead voices.
> VLADIMIR: They make a noise like wings.
> ESTRAGON: Like leaves.
> VLADIMIR: Like sand.
> ESTRAGON: Like leaves.
>   *Silence.*
> VLADIMIR: They all speak at once.

ESTRAGON: Each one to itself.
  Silence.
VLADIMIR: Rather they whisper.
ESTRAGON: They rustle.
VLADIMIR: They murmur.
ESTRAGON: They rustle.
  Silence.
VLADIMIR: What do they say?
ESTRAGON: They talk about their lives.
VLADIMIR: To have lived is not enough for them.
ESTRAGON: They have to talk about it.
VLADIMIR: To be dead is not enough for them.
ESTRAGON: It is not sufficient.
  Silence.
VLADIMIR: They make a noise like feathers.
ESTRAGON: Like leaves.
VLADIMIR: Like ashes.
ESTRAGON: Like leaves.
  Long silence.
VLADIMIR: Say something!

It is the ultimate, dark transumption of Shelley's fiction of the leaves in the apocalyptic "Ode to the West Wind." Involuntary Gnostics, Estragon and Vladimir are beyond apocalypse, beyond any hope for this world. A tree may bud overnight, but this is not so much like an early miracle (as Kenner says) as it is "another of your nightmares" (as Estragon says). The reentry of the blinded Pozzo, now reduced to crying "Help!" is the drama's most poignant moment, even as its most dreadful negation is shouted by blind Pozzo in his fury, after Vladimir asks a temporal question once too often:

POZZO: (*suddenly furious*). Have you not done tormenting
  me with your accursed time! It's abominable! When!
  When! One day, is that not enough for you, one
  day he went dumb, one day I went blind, one day
  we'll go deaf, one day we were born, one day we
  shall die, the same day, the same second, is that not
  enough for you? (*Calmer.*) They give birth astride
  of a grave, the light gleams an instant, then it's
  night once more.

Pozzo, originally enough of a brute to be a Demiurge himself, is now another wanderer in the darkness of the *kenoma*. Estragon's dreadful question, as to whether Pozzo may not have been Godot, is answered negatively by Vladimir, but with something less than perfect confidence. Despite the boy's later testimony, I suspect that the tragicomedy centers precisely there: in the possible identity of Godot and Pozzo, in the unhappy intimation that the Demiurge is not only the god of this world, the spirit of Schopenhauer's Will to Live, but the only god that can be uncovered anywhere, even anywhere out of this world.

Bailing Out the Silence

John Fletcher

One evening, on a lonely country road near a tree, two elderly men, half tramp half clown, are waiting for someone of the name of Godot who has, they believe, given them to understand that their patience at the rendezvous will be rewarded. The two, Estragon ("Gogo") and Vladimir ("Didi"), are not sure what form Godot's gratitude will take, any more than they know for certain whether they have come to the right place on the appointed day. They occupy the time as best they can until distraction arrives in the shape of Pozzo, a local landowner on his way to the fair to sell his slave Lucky. Pozzo halts awhile with Estragon and Vladimir, eats his lunch in their presence, even grants them his bones when his menial spurns them, and then in gratitude for their society has Lucky dance and then think aloud for them. The three become so agitated by Lucky's intellectual performance that they all set upon him and silence him. Not long afterwards Pozzo takes his leave, driving Lucky before him. Estragon and Vladimir have not been alone many moments together before a small boy appears with the news that Mr Godot "won't come this evening but surely tomorrow." The boy departs, night falls abruptly, and after briefly contemplating suicide by hanging themselves from the tree, the two men decide to call it a day, but despite their decision to go, do not move as the curtain falls.

The curtain rises the next day on a scene identical except for the fact that the tree has sprouted a few leaves. Vladimir is joined on stage by Estragon and much the same things happen, except that

From *Beckett: A Study of His Plays.* © 1972, 1978, 1985, 1987 by John Fletcher. Methuen, 1972.

when Pozzo and Lucky appear (from the side they made their exit from in act 1), Pozzo turns out to have gone blind and Lucky dumb. After all four collapse on top of each other and then somehow manage to get up again, Pozzo becomes exasperated at Vladimir's questions about time, bellowing that life itself is only a brief instant. He leaves, driving Lucky before him, from the side he had entered from in act 1. After another brief interval the boy comes on a second time and delivers the same message as before. The sun sets, the moon rises abruptly, the two men again contemplate suicide, but without much determination, and then, despite their agreement to leave, make no movement as the curtain falls. So ends the play in which, as one critic wittily but inaccurately put it, nothing happens, twice.

Perhaps the most striking thing about Beckett's second work for the stage is its maturity. This impression springs mainly from the fact that it is a convincingly created dramatic image, that the dialogue is ably constructed and the characterization effectively conceived. It is to some extent a misleading impression, however, since the text now available was established only after a number of versions had been tried out. The original French manuscript is still unpublished, but enough is known about it to show that it was a rather hesitant piece of work: Beckett was not sure what names to give his characters, for instance, and even whether or not to make Godot a real presence in the action by suggesting, for instance, that Estragon and Vladimir have a written assignation with him, or that Pozzo himself is Godot failing to recognize those he has come to meet. These matters were settled in the first French edition which preceded Roger Blin's creation by a few months, but even this text differs in certain respects from the second, post-performance edition. In production, moreover, Blin advised certain cuts for reasons of technical effectiveness, and at that stage in his dramatic career Beckett was only too ready to learn from a professional. When he undertook the first English translation, therefore, he dropped most of the passages Blin leaves out, and then, in the definitive edition of 1965, not only seized the opportunity of restoring the Lord Chamberlain's censored passages, but also of making a large number of minor amendments to the dialogue and directions which considerably enhance the play's theatrical effectiveness. So that the text we now possess has gone through a considerable polishing process in manuscript and in print, both on the stage and off it. When we recall that this development has taken place over a period of some fifteen years, the transition from the jettisoned *Eleuthéria* is not as abrupt as might at first sight appear. Although the first draft of *Godot* was written quickly, in a matter of just over three months, the way had been prepared for it by *Eleuthéria* as well as other Beckett works. We have noted that the model for Vladimir's exchanges with Godot's boy-messenger lay in the glazier's conversations in the earlier play; detailed analyses have revealed close similarities between the novel *Mercier et Camier* and *Waiting for Godot;* and as we saw [elsewhere], Beckett himself has said that the play's origins may be sought in *Murphy*.

Of course, *Waiting for Godot* also has its antecedents within the broader context of the post-naturalist tradition. A few of the analogues that have been cited are Strindberg's *Dream Play*, with its sense of repetitiveness and unreality, Synge's *The Well of the Saints,* Jarry's *Ubu* cycle (Pozzo is distinctly ubuesque), Vitrac's *Victor; or, The Children Take Over,* not to mention the classic Chaplin who developed his astonishing persona after observing the gait of a drunken cabby. And Beckett is close, naturally, to another great poet of inertia, Chekhov. Their plays share a feeling of inconclusiveness: apart from the sale of the estate, for example, nothing much can be said to happen in *The Cherry Orchard*. The heroine goes back to her unsatisfactory lover in Paris, other characters turn again to their idle dreams, and the proposal of marriage which Varia had been hoping Lopahin would make her does not materialize. Frustrations and a sense of impotence felt by many of the characters provoke tensions between them, and lead to the occasional eruption which subsides as suddenly as similar explosions of anger between Vladimir and Estragon. A forced gaiety in most of Chekhov's characters masks an awareness of abandonment and hopelessness experienced by them; none the less, like Beckett's, they continue to hope unrealistically for a better world just over the hill. Both dramatists excel in laying bare both the nature of life without real hope of improvement or change, and the subterfuges we adopt to conceal from ourselves the worst facts about our condition, in dialogue that modulates with striking rapidity from the sublime to the ridiculous, speech without consequence reflecting action without conclusion. In spite of all, indeed, both Chekhov and Beckett offer us a subdued form of comedy to illustrate Nell's profound dictum in *Endgame:* "Nothing is funnier than unhappiness . . . It's the most comical thing in the world," since to laugh at our misery is the only way we have found of coming to terms with it. *Waiting for Godot* shows parallels, too, with some of Yeats's plays. In *The Cat and the Moon* of 1926, for example, two beggars, one halt and the other sightless, have for years managed to compensate their respective infirmities by the blind man carrying the lame man on his back. But these and others are largely fortuitous congruences, facts of theatre history to be accorded no more than their due, which is to reveal that *Waiting for Godot* does not stand in splendid isolation.

In several ways, indeed, it is a somewhat traditional play. As spectators we are, for example, launched directly into the action, *in medias res,* and the relatively few details we need for comprehension of the past career of the characters are filled in for us as we go along. Vladimir's "So there you are again" assumes a previous history of association between himself and Estragon which the spectator, perfectly normally, takes on trust. The time scale, too, is clearly theatrical rather than actual. When Vladimir, only a few minutes in real time after his entry in act 2, says of Lucky's hat, "I've been here an hour and never saw it," Beckett is using one of the oldest dramaturgical tricks for suggesting greater duration than has in fact elapsed.

It is often said that the new forms of drama which arose in the 1950s, and of which *Waiting for Godot* is so outstandingly representative, flout all the rules of traditional dramaturgy. To an extent this is true enough; but it is also a fact that more recent developments, particularly in the field of improvisatory drama and the happening, have outstripped the earlier avant-garde, revealing how even in its anti-rhetoric it still preserved rhetoric, and how zealously it maintained the hallowed distinction between stage and auditorium. I shall have more to say about the rhetoric of *Godot* later; but the sense of being in a theatre *qua* theatre is certainly something the play relies upon implicitly. Just imagine what would happen if a member of the audience took it into his head to cross the footlights and join in the delicately orchestrated banter between the characters! The effect would be the same as on the notorious occasion when an outraged spectator felt impelled to warn Othello against the machinations of Iago. The existential divide between the two worlds of actors and theatregoers is even, in this play, dwelt on with coy jocularity. With his gesture of gazing into the wings, "his hand screening his eyes," Estragon is being absurdly theatrical, as he is also in his unflatteringly ironic comment about "inspiring prospects" when looking the audience pointedly in the eyes a little later. Vladimir situates one of the local landmarks, a bog, in the auditorium, and comically sympathizes with Estragon's hesitation in act 2 to take cover by running in that direction, despite the fact that "there's not a soul in sight." Pozzo in particular shows an old pro's awareness of where he should be: "It isn't by any chance the place known as the Board?" he asks in act 2. The play's perfect sense of theatre can thus be explained partly in terms of its self-conscious awareness of theatre.

But it is also attributable in part to Beckett's fine ear for eminently actable dialogue, once the problem of the frequent occurrence of virtually identical cues has been overcome in rehearsal. The vividly conjugal bickering of Vladimir and Estragon is a case in point. Vladimir is the anxious type, and Estragon shows few scruples about needling him where he is most vulnerable. "What are you insinuating," Vladimir asks in some alarm, "that we've come to the wrong place?" as Estragon proceeds to undermine his confidence. His companion continues mercilessly insidious in his questions: "But what Saturday? And is it Saturday? Is it not rather Sunday? Or Monday? Or Friday?" He soon tires of this, however, and leaves Vladimir with his cruel dilemma about whether they have turned up on the right day and at the right place for their appointment with Godot. He is impatient in a general way with Vladimir's restlessness, his habit of waking him from his catnaps, his slowness in grasping points of logic ("Use your intelligence, can't you?" he barks when Vladimir fails to see why the heavier of the two should be the first to attempt suicide by hanging from a dubious branch). On a more brutal level, Pozzo torments Lucky with a calculatedly sadistic brand of boorishness and feigned commiseration. As for the language Estragon and Vladimir use when addressing Pozzo, this varies from the timorously respectful in the first act to the familiarly condescending in the second. In every case the language shows a pithy accuracy and liveliness, with a touch of Dublinese ("get up till I embrace you" is a typical Irishism), but otherwise lacking in distracting provincialisms: a universal form of English speech that is characteristic of Beckett's international background and of the fact that his play was conceived in a perfectly fluent French before it was recast in the author's mother tongue.

The dialogue none the less shows certain features which are characteristic of Beckett's manner as we have come to know it through increasing familiarity with the style of his prose written both for armchair reading and for stage performance. One of these verbal tics is the device of cancellation or qualification, which seems to stem from a deep-seated scepticism about the medium of language itself. Molloy, for instance, says of a man he has been observing, "A little dog followed him, a pomeranian I think, but I don't think so" (*Three Novels*), without showing himself in the least perturbed by the *volte-face*. Similarly with Vladimir, who twice qualifies his admission of ignorance about the nature of the tree: "I don't know," he asserts, adding at once, "A willow." An analogous hesitation perhaps explains why some of the play's many questions, which make up twenty-four percent of all utterances according to Barry Smith, terminate in a full stop rather than a question mark, so that it is hardly surprising that replies account for only twelve percent of all remarks. But questions diffidently put are one thing; questions long held in suspense, like "We're not tied?" or not answered at all, such as "Like to finish it?" are another thing altogether. Estragon, for instance, is promised an account of "the time Lucky refused" by Pozzo, who has said enigmatically and menacingly "He refused once," but the hope of further information on this score, as on others, is cheated. Much of the dialogue, in fact, simulates the inconsequential spontaneity of everyday speech, in which the different participants tend to pursue a line of thought independently of each other—a technique which Harold Pinter, in particular, has raised to the level of high art. Beckett counterpoints resulting misunderstandings with comic subtlety, as in this exchange, which precedes Lucky's speech:

POZZO: Gentlemen, you have been . . . civil to me.
ESTRAGON: Not at all.
VLADIMIR: What an idea!
POZZO: Yes yes, you have been correct. So that I ask myself is there anything I can do in my turn for these honest fellows who are having such a dull, dull time.
ESTRAGON: Even ten francs would be welcome.
VLADIMIR: We are not beggars!
POZZO: Is there anything I can do, that's what I ask myself, to cheer them up? I have given them bones, I have talked to them about this and that, I have explained the twilight, admittedly. But is it enough, that's what tortures me, is it enough?
ESTRAGON: Even five.

VLADIMIR: That's enough!

ESTRAGON: I couldn't accept less.

POZZO: Is it enough? No doubt. But I am liberal. It's my
    nature. This evening. So much the worse for me.
    For I shall suffer, no doubt about that. What do
    you prefer? Shall we have him dance, or sing, or
    recite, or think, or—

ESTRAGON: Who?

POZZO: Who! You know how to think, you two?

VLADIMIR: He thinks?

POZZO: Certainly. Aloud.

Such comic misunderstandings are pure vaudeville: "I must have thrown them away—When?—I don't know.—Why?—I don't know why I don't know?" is another typical example. But even here the language is rooted in common speech, in which time is lost through confusions over the precise meaning of words. "Are you friends?" blind Pozzo asks in act 2, provoking Estragon to noisy laughter: "He wants to know if we are friends!" Vladimir mediates here as on other occasions by pointing out, "No, he means friends of his." The dialogue owes a great deal in fact to the classic stichomythia of music hall cross-talk routines, in which a "straight" man is placed opposite a "funny" man who delights the audience by becoming embroiled in the complexities of some problem his partner is attempting, with diminishing patience, to elucidate for his benefit. In this play, as we have seen, Estragon tries to explain to Vladimir that since he is the heavier of the two he should logically try hanging himself from the bough first: "if it hangs you it'll hang anything," he concludes with some exasperation. The comedy of this is reinforced when the initial premise itself is brought into question: "But am I heavier than you?" asks Vladimir, who is usually cast as a thin and nervous man opposite Estragon's stouter and more turgid physique. Another well-worn music-hall gag is mirrored repetition: both Estragon and Vladimir, for example, almost simultaneously shake and feel about inside a favourite object, Vladimir his hat, and Estragon his boot, and both men exclaim histrionically "Hurts! He wants to know if it hurts!" within a minute of each other. This last joke follows the pattern of so many rhetorical appeals to the audience of the following type: "Thin? I'd say my wife is thin. When she swallowed a pickled onion whole, the neighbours started talking" (quoted by Benny

Green in *Radio Times,* 23 April 1970). Estragon is equally knowing in this characteristic piece of cross talk:

> ESTRAGON: And we?
> VLADIMIR: I beg your pardon?
> ESTRAGON: I said, And we?
> VLADIMIR: I don't understand.
> ESTRAGON: Where do we come in?
> VLADIMIR: Come in?
> ESTRAGON: Take your time.

Another form of music hall comedy was the monologue, which Dan Leno and Arthur English made their specialty: in this play it is Pozzo who practises the art, in his disquisition on the twilight which terminates gloomily, "That's how it is on this bitch of an earth," as well as—of course more sombrely—in his tirade in act 2 about life taking up but an instant as "they give birth astride of a grave." But Vladimir too has his set pieces, for instance the comic banter which begins, "Let us not waste our time in idle discourse!" and proceeds to do just that.

The circus is another source of *Godot's* unique brand of humour. Anouilh likened the play to the *Thoughts* of Pascal performed as a comedy sketch for clowns. Certainly the totters, the pratfalls, the tumbles, Estragon's trouser dropping, Vladimir's duck waddle, Lucky's palsy and Pozzo's cracking of his ringmaster's whip are all lifted straight from the repertoire of the big top. The amount of gesture in a play reputedly actionless is in fact extraordinary. Estragon and Vladimir, for instance, entertain themselves and their audience at one moment by swapping hats in a complex routine which leaves Vladimir significantly in possession of Lucky's, the source of the menial's eloquence. The hats themselves are a direct tribute to the masters of silent-film comedy, Chaplin and Keaton, and their talkie successors Laurel and Hardy. All of this (music-hall patter, circus clowning and movie costume) is taken, even down to the round song and the lullaby which Vladimir offers us, from the most popular and unpretentious forms of entertainment, where what is lacking in subtlety and finesse is made up for in well-drilled smoothness and in perfection of timing. Like such cruder art forms, this play must be well paced if it is to succeed: the bursts of action or of verbal ping-pong must really move, and the indicated silences which punctuate them must be genuinely palpable halts. If this is done, the play's characteristic rhythm comes forcibly across, and reveals not only the wit, but also the sheer entertainment that resides in a work unjustly thought of as gloomy and boring. How can a play like this be dull, if Estragon's priceless howler (in asking a question answered pages before) is delivered as it should be, with an old trouper's exact sense of timing? Or if Pozzo's words and actions are exploited as they should be, by an actor with the requisite presence and physique which the role cries out for? Far from weakening or trivializing the work, a director who brings its comic elements out accurately enables the play's serious meditation on the vanity of human wishes to be made all the more forcibly.

The vital thing for any production of this play to achieve, in fact, is a proper tautness. It may not be constructed along traditional lines, with exposition, development, peripeteia and dénouement, but it *has* a firm structure, albeit of a different kind, a structure based on repetition, the return of leitmotifs, and on the exact balancing of variable elements, and it is this structure which must be brought out in production. The sort of repetition the audience must be conditioned to respond to can be seen in the following example. Pozzo, having eaten his meal and lit his pipe, says with evident satisfaction, "Ah! That's better." Two pages later Estragon makes precisely the same comment, having just gnawed the remaining flesh off Pozzo's discarded chicken bones. But the circumstances, though similar, are not identical: Pozzo has fed to satiety, Estragon has made a meagre repast of his leavings. The repetition of the words in different mouths is therefore an ironical device for pointing a contrast, like that between Pozzo's selfish bellow "Coat!" to Lucky in act 1, and Vladimir's selfless spreading of *his* coat round Estragon's shoulders in act 2.

The entire movement of the play, therefore, depends on balance. "It is the shape that matters" Beckett once remarked apropos of the Augustinian saying which underlies so much of the play's symbolism: "Do not despair—one of the thieves was saved; do not presume—one of the thieves was damned." It is certainly the shape that matters here: the director must bring out the "stylized movement" which Beckett himself stressed in discussion with Charles Marowitz, a movement which relies heavily on asymmetry, or repetition with a difference. In both acts, for instance, Pozzo's arrival is curiously foreshadowed by one of the men imagining he hears sounds of people approaching; and whereas in the first act the two prop Lucky up, in the second they serve as "caryatids" to Pozzo. But the most poignant example is the ending of the two sections, where the wording is identical, the punctuation varied only slightly to slow down delivery the second time, but the roles reversed: in act 1 Estragon asks the question, but act 2 gives it to Vladimir:

> VLADIMIR: Well? Shall we go?
> ESTRAGON: Yes, let's go.

The first time round, these two sentences can be delivered at more or less normal speed, but on the second occasion they should be drawn out, with three- to six-second pauses between their constituent phrases. When this is done, the intense emotion generated in the auditorium as the last curtain falls is redolent of great sadness.

But the asymmetrical reproduction of nearly everything in two acts of unequal length is not the only structural feature in the play. Another is the manner in which the counterpointing of the act-structure is mirrored in the contrasted characterization. Estragon's name is composed of the same number of letters as Vladimir's; the same applies to Pozzo and Lucky. Hence they find themselves associated, and have been joined in a complex sadomasochistic relationship for many years. But their natures obviously conflict: Vladimir is the neurotic intellectual type, Estragon the placid intuitive sort; Pozzo is the bullying extravert, Lucky the timorous introvert. Vladimir instinctively sympathizes with Lucky, and for Pozzo Estragon experiences a degree of fellow-feeling. Vladimir and Pozzo, like Lucky and Estragon who kick each other, are at the extremes of the poised poles. Estragon is afraid of being "tied," Lucky is tied in effect; Vladimir kowtows to authority, Pozzo asserts it forcibly. The characters, in fact, like the occurrences both major and minor, are held in uneasy equilibrium within this play.

Yet another of its structural features is the way the writing modulates continually from one tone to its opposite. Pozzo's declamation on the night, for instance, shifts almost violently from the false sublime to the prosaically ridiculous, and after rising to "vibrant" heights lapses to "gloomy" depths, and ultimately to inevitable silence. After a long pause, Estragon and Vladimir strike up and swap vaudeville remarks:

> ESTRAGON: So long as one knows.
> VLADIMIR: One can bide one's time.
> ESTRAGON: One knows what to expect.

VLADIMIR: No further need to worry.
ESTRAGON: Simply wait.
VLADIMIR: We're used to it.

The transition is masterly, almost musical in subtlety, like the sound of the strings when the brass dies away. Similar modulation occurs between the high jinks of the business around Lucky in act 1 and the high grief of Vladimir's cross-examination of the Boy in act 2, culminating in the great cry from the mass, "Christ have mercy on us!" Farce and pathos are closely mingled throughout, but perhaps most obviously at the start of act 2 in the clowns' loving embrace which ends, appropriately, in a grotesque pratfall.

The whole of act 2, in fact, shows a slightly different tone from act 1. The cross talk is of a more "intellectual" and less overtly music-hall kind; the confident Pozzo of the first act is changed into the sightless decrepit of act 2; and the words of the Boy, delivered "in a rush" in act 1, have to be dragged out of him by Vladimir the second time round. The entire second panel of this diptych is less naturalistic, and assumes familiarity with the two down-and-outs and their ways which permits a briefer restatement of the theme. Pozzo enters later, and is sooner gone. Lucky's monologue of act 1, despite its repetitious and garbled jargon, made a point: that man, notwithstanding the existence of a caring god of sorts and progress of various kinds, is in full decline; even this statement from a degraded man of reason cannot recur in act 2, because, we learn with terror, he has gone dumb.

Lucky's speech, however, like so much else in the play, is calculatedly deceptive if we expect it to yield a significant key to the work as a whole. Those who are perplexed by the play's "meaning" may draw at least some comfort from the author's assurance that it means what it says, neither more nor less. It is perhaps easier to accept this, now that his other works are better known; easier indeed than fifteen years ago, when it was not so evident that Beckett is no didactic writer concerned to put across a "message" in dramatic form. Even the many Christian echoes in the play must now be seen to add up not to any coherent religious statement, but rather to a meditation upon a world governed by no other divinity than some sort of malignant fate; a world in which man waits and hopes for something to give value to his life and distract him from the absurdity of his death. "For there comes the hour," Malone writes, "when nothing more can happen and nobody more can come and all is ended but the waiting that knows itself in vain" (*Three Novels*). It is a diffuse awareness of this which informs the bickering, the histrionics and the horseplay of *Waiting for Godot*, a meditative rhapsody on the nullity of human attainment written for performance by an ever-hopeful troupe of circus clowns, bailing out the silence from a sinking ship of a play which is Beckett's magnificently rebellious gesture to an art form he then proceeds to disrupt and transcend.

The Search for the Self

Martin Esslin

On November 19, 1957, a group of worried actors were preparing to face their audience. The actors were members of the company of the San Francisco Actors' Workshop. The audience consisted of fourteen hundred convicts at the San Quentin penitentiary. No live play had been performed at San Quentin since Sarah Bernhardt appeared there in 1913. Now, forty-four years later, the play that had been chosen, largely because no woman appeared in it, was Samuel Beckett's *Waiting for Godot*.

No wonder the actors and Herbert Blau, the director, were apprehensive. How were they to face one of the toughest audiences in the world with a highly obscure, intellectual play that had produced near riots among a good many highly sophisticated audiences in Western Europe? Herbert Blau decided to prepare the San Quentin audience for what was to come. He stepped on to the stage and addressed the packed, darkened North Dining Hall—a sea of flickering matches that the convicts tossed over their shoulders after lighting their cigarettes. Blau compared the play to a piece of jazz music "to which one must listen for whatever one may find in it." In the same way, he hoped, there would be some meaning, some personal significance for each member of the audience in *Waiting for Godot*.

The curtain parted. The play began. And what had bewildered the sophisticated audiences of Paris, London, and New York was

From *The Theatre of the Absurd*. © 1961, 1968, 1969 by Martin Esslin. Overlook Press, 1973.

immediately grasped by an audience of convicts. As the writer of "Memos of a first-nighter" put it in the columns of the prison paper, the *San Quentin News:*

> The trio of muscle-men, biceps overflowing, . . . parked all 642 lbs on the aisle and waited for the girls and funny stuff. When this didn't appear they audibly fumed and audibly decided to wait until the house lights dimmed before escaping. They made one error. They listened and looked two minutes too long—and stayed. Left at the end. All shook.

Or as the writer of the lead story of the same paper reported, under the headline, "San Francisco Group Leaves S.Q. Audience Waiting for Godot":

> From the moment Robin Wagner's thoughtful and limbo-like set was dressed with light, until the last futile and expectant handclasp was hesitantly activated between the two searching vagrants, the San Francisco company had its audience of captives in its collective hand. . . . Those that had felt a less controversial vehicle should be attempted as a first play here had their fears allayed a short five minutes after the Samuel Beckett piece began to unfold.

A reporter from the San Francisco *Chronicle* who was present noted that the convicts did not find it difficult to understand the play. One prisoner told him, "Godot is society." Said another, "He's the outside." A teacher at the prison was quoted as saying, "They know what is meant by waiting . . . and they knew if Godot finally came, he would only be a disappointment." The leading article of the prison paper showed how clearly the writer had understood the meaning of the play:

> It was an expression, symbolic in order to avoid all personal error, by an author who expected each member of his audience to draw his own conclusions, make his own errors. It asked nothing in point, it forced no dramatized moral on the viewer, it held out no specific hope. . . . We're still waiting for Godot, and shall continue to wait. When the scenery gets too drab and the action too slow, we'll call each other names and swear to part forever—but then, there's no place to go!

It is said that Godot himself, as well as turns of phrase and characters from the play, have since become a permanent part of the private language, the institutional mythology of San Quentin.

Why did a play of the supposedly esoteric avant-garde make so immediate and so deep an impact on an audience of convicts? Because it confronted them with a situation in some ways analogous to their own? Perhaps. Or perhaps because they were unsophisticated enough to come to the theatre without any preconceived notions and ready-made expectations, so that they avoided the mistake that trapped so many established critics who condemned the play for its lack of plot, development, characterization, suspense, or plain common sense. Certainly the prisoners of San Quentin could not be suspected of the sin of intellectual snobbery, for which a sizeable proportion of the audiences of *Waiting for Godot* have often been reproached; of pretending to like a play they did not even begin to understand, just to appear in the know.

The reception of *Waiting for Godot* at San Quentin, and the wide acclaim given to plays by Ionesco, Adamov, Pinter, and others, testify that these plays, which are so often superciliously dismissed as nonsense or mystification, *have* something to say and *can* be understood. Most of the incomprehension with which plays of this type are still being received by critics and theatrical reviewers, most of the bewilderment they have caused and to which they still give rise, come from the fact that they are part of a new, and still developing stage convention that has not yet been generally understood and has hardly ever been defined. Inevitably, plays written in this new convention will, when judged by the standards and criteria of another, be regarded as impertinent and outrageous impostures. If a good play must have a cleverly constructed story, these have no story or plot to speak of; if a good play is judged by subtlety of characterization and motivation, these are often without recognizable characters and present the audience with almost mechanical puppets; if a good play has to have a fully explained theme, which is neatly exposed and finally solved, these often have neither a beginning nor an end; if a good play is to hold the mirror up to nature and portray the manners and mannerisms of the age in finely observed sketches, these seem often to be reflections of dreams and nightmares; if a good play relies on witty repartee and pointed dialogue, these often consist of incoherent babblings.

But the plays we are concerned with here pursue ends quite

different from those of the conventional play and therefore use quite different methods. They can be judged only by the standards of the Theatre of the Absurd. . . .

When Alan Schneider, who was to direct the first American production of *Waiting for Godot,* asked Beckett who or what was meant by Godot, he received the answer, "If I knew, I would have said so in the play."

This is a salutary warning to anyone who approaches Beckett's plays with the intention of discovering *the* key to their understanding, of demonstrating in exact and definite terms *what they mean.* Such an undertaking might perhaps be justified in tackling the works of an author who had started from a clear-cut philosophical or moral conception, and had then proceeded to translate it into concrete terms of plot and character. But even in such a case the chances are that the final product, if it turned out a genuine work of the creative imagination, would transcend the author's original intentions and present itself as far richer, more complex, and open to a multitude of additional interpretations. For, as Beckett himself has pointed out in his essay on Joyce's *Work in Progress,* the form, structure, and mood of an artistic statement cannot be separated from its meaning, its conceptual content; simply because the work of art as a whole *is* its meaning, *what* is said in it is indissolubly linked with the *manner* in which it is said, and cannot be said in any other way. Libraries have been filled with attempts to reduce the meaning of a play like *Hamlet* to a few short and simple lines, yet the play itself remains the clearest and most concise statement of its meaning and message, precisely because its uncertainties and irreducible ambiguities are an essential element of its total impact.

These considerations apply, in varying degrees, to all works of creative literature, but they apply with particular force to works that are essentially concerned with conveying their author's sense of mystery, bewilderment, and anxiety when confronted with the human condition, and his despair at being unable to find a meaning in existence. In *Waiting for Godot,* the feeling of uncertainty it produces, the ebb and flow of this uncertainty—from the hope of discovering the identity of Godot to its repeated disappointment—are themselves the essence of the play. Any endeavour to arrive at a clear and certain interpretation by establishing the identity of Godot through critical analysis would be as foolish as trying to discover the clear outlines hidden behind the chiaroscuro of a painting by Rembrandt by scraping away the paint.

Yet it is only natural that plays written in so unusual and baffling a convention should be felt to be in special need of an explanation that, as it were, would uncover their hidden meaning and translate it into everyday language. The source of this fallacy lies in the misconception that somehow these plays must be reducible to the conventions of the "normal" theatre, with plots that can be summarized in the form of a narrative. If only one could discover some hidden clue, it is felt, these difficult plays could be forced to yield their secret and reveal the plot of the conventional play that is hidden within them. Such attempts are doomed to failure. Beckett's plays lack plot even more completely than other works of the Theatre of the Absurd. Instead of a linear development, they present their author's intuition of the human condition by a method that is essentially polyphonic; they confront their audience with an organized structure of statements and images that interpenetrate each other and that must be apprehended in their totality, rather like the different themes in a symphony, which gain meaning by their simultaneous interaction.

But if we have to be cautious in our approach to Beckett's plays, to avoid the pitfall of trying to provide an oversimplified explanation of their meaning, this does not imply that we cannot subject them to careful scrutiny by isolating sets of images and themes and by attempting to discern their structural groundwork. The results of such an examination should make it easier to follow the author's intention and to see, if not the *answers* to his questions, at least what the *questions* are that he is asking.

Waiting for Godot does not tell a story; it explores a static situation. "Nothing happens, nobody comes, nobody goes, it's awful." On a country road, by a tree, two old tramps, Vladimir and Estragon, are waiting. That is the opening situation at the beginning of act 1. At the end of act 1 they are informed that Mr Godot, with whom they believe they have an appointment, cannot come, but that he will surely come tomorrow. Act 2 repeats precisely the same pattern. The same boy arrives and delivers the same message. Act 1 ends:

> ESTRAGON: Well, shall we go?
> VLADIMIR: Yes, let's go.
> *They do not move.*

Act 2 ends with the same lines of dialogue, but spoken by the same characters in reversed order.

The sequence of events and the dialogue in each act are different. Each time the two tramps encounter another pair of characters, Pozzo and Lucky, master and slave, under differing circumstances; in each act Vladimir and Estragon attempt suicide and fail, for differing reasons; but these variations merely serve to emphasize the essential sameness of the situation—*plus ça change, plus c'est la même chose.*

Vladimir and Estragon—who call each other Didi and Gogo, although Vladimir is addressed by the boy messenger as Mr Albert, and Estragon, when asked his name, replies without hesitation, Catullus—are clearly derived from the pairs of cross-talk comedians of music halls. Their dialogue has the peculiar repetitive quality of the cross-talk comedians' patter.

> ESTRAGON: SO LONG AS ONE KNOWS.
> VLADIMIR: One can bide one's time.
> ESTRAGON: One knows what to expect.
> VLADIMIR: No further need to worry.

And the parallel to the music hall and the circus is even explicitly stated:

> VLADIMIR: Charming evening we're having.
> ESTRAGON: Unforgettable.
> VLADIMIR: And it's not over.
> ESTRAGON: Apparently not.
> VLADIMIR: It's only the beginning.
> ESTRAGON: It's awful
> VLADIMIR: It's worse than being at the theatre.
> ESTRAGON: The circus.
> VLADIMIR: The music hall.
> ESTRAGON: The circus.

In accordance with the traditions of the music hall or the circus, there is an element of crudely physical humor: Estragon loses his trousers, there is a protracted gag involving three hats that are put on and off and handed on in a sequence of seemingly unending confusion, and there is an abundance of pratfalls—the writer of a penetrating thesis on Beckett, Niklaus Gessner, lists no fewer than forty-five stage directions indicating that one of the characters leaves the upright position, which symbolizes the dignity of man.

As the members of a cross-talk act, Vladimir and Estragon have complementary personalities. Vladimir is the more practical of the two, and Estragon claims to have been a poet. In eating his carrot, Estragon finds that the more he eats of it the less he likes it, while Vladimir reacts the opposite way—he likes things as he gets used to them. Estragon is volatile, Vladimir persistent. Estragon dreams, Vladimir cannot stand hearing about dreams. Vladimir has stinking breath, Estragon has stinking feet. Vladimir remembers past events, Estragon tends to forget them as soon as they have happened. Estragon likes telling funny stories, Vladimir is upset by them. It is mainly Vladimir who voices the hope that Godot will come and that his coming will change their situation, while Estragon remains sceptical throughout and at times even forgets the name of Godot. It is Vladimir who conducts the conversation with the boy who is Godot's messenger and to whom the boy's messages are addressed. Estragon is the weaker of the two; he is beaten up by mysterious strangers every night. Vladimir at times acts as his protector, sings him to sleep with a lullaby, and covers him with his coat. The opposition of their temperaments is the cause of endless bickering between them and often leads to the suggestion that they should part. Yet, being complementary natures, they also are dependent on each other and have to stay together.

Pozzo and Lucky are equally complementary in their natures, but their relationship is on a more primitive level: Pozzo is the sadistic master, Lucky the submissive slave. In the first act, Pozzo is rich, powerful, and certain of himself; he represents worldly man in all his facile and shortsighted optimism and illusory feeling of power and permanence. Lucky not only carries his heavy luggage, and even the whip with which Pozzo beats him, he also dances and thinks for him, or did so in his prime. In fact, Lucky taught Pozzo all the higher values of life: "beauty, grace, truth of the first water." Pozzo and Lucky represent the relationship between body and mind, the material and the spiritual sides of man, with the intellect subordinate to the appetites of the body. Now that Lucky's powers are failing, Pozzo complains that they cause him untold suffering. He wants to get rid of Lucky and sell him at the fair. But in the second act, when they appear again, they are still tied together. Pozzo has gone blind, Lucky has become dumb. While Pozzo drives Lucky on a journey without an apparent goal, Vladimir has prevailed upon Estragon to wait for Godot.

A good deal of ingenuity has been expended in trying to establish at least an etymology for Godot's name, which would point to Beckett's conscious or subconscious intention in making him the objective of Vladimir's and Estragon's quest. It has been suggested that Godot is a weakened form of the word "God," a diminutive formed on the analogy of Pierre-Pierrot, Charles-Charlot, with the added association of the Charlie Chaplin character of the little man, who is called Charlot in France, and whose bowler hat is worn by all four main characters in the play. It has also been noted that the title *En attendant Godot* seems to contain an allusion to Simone Weil's book *Attente de Dieu,* which would furnish a further indication that Godot stands for God. Yet the name Godot may also be an even more recondite literary allusion. As Eric Bentley has pointed out, there is a character in a play by Balzac, a character much talked about but never seen, and called Godeau. The play in question is Balzac's comedy *Le Faiseur,* better known as *Mercadet.* Mercadet is a stock exchange speculator who is in the habit of attributing his financial difficulties to his former partner Godeau, who, years before, absconded with their joint capital: *"Je porte le poids du crime de Godeau!"* On the other hand, the hope of Godeau's eventual return and the repayment of the embezzled funds is constantly dangled by Mercadet before the eyes of his numerous creditors. *"Tout le monde a son Godeau, un faux Christophe Colomb! Après tout Godeau . . . je crois qu'il m'a déjà rapporté plus d'argent qu'il ne m'en a pris!"* The plot of *Mercadet* turns on a last, desperate speculation based on the appearance of a spurious Godeau. But the fraud is discovered. Mercadet seems ruined. At this moment the real Godeau is announced; he has returned from India with a huge fortune. The play ends with Mercadet exclaiming, *"J'ai montré tant de fois Godeau que j'ai bien le droit de le voir. Allons voir Godeau!"*

The parallels are too striking to make it probable that this is a mere coincidence. In Beckett's play, as in Balzac's, the arrival of Godot is the eagerly awaited event that will miraculously save the situation; and Beckett is as fond as Joyce of subtle and recondite literary allusions.

Yet whether Godot is meant to suggest the intervention of a supernatural agency, or whether he stands for a mythical human being whose arrival is expected to change the situation, or both of these possibilities combined, his exact nature is of secondary importance. The subject of the play is not Godot but waiting, the act of waiting as an essential and characteristic aspect of the human condition. Throughout our lives we always wait for something, and Godot simply represents the objective of our waiting—an event, a thing, a person, death. Moreover, it is in the act of waiting that we experience the flow of *time* in its purest, most evident form. If we are active, we tend to forget the passage of time, we *pass* the time, but if we are merely passively waiting, we are confronted with the action of time itself. As Beckett points out in his analysis of Proust, "There is no escape from the hours and the days. Neither from tomorrow nor from yesterday because yesterday has deformed us, or been deformed by us. . . . Yesterday is not a milestone that has been passed, but a daystone on the beaten track of the years, and irremediably part of us, within us, heavy and dangerous. We are not merely more weary because of yesterday, we are other, no longer what we were before the calamity of yesterday." The flow of time confronts us with the basic problem of being—the problem of the nature of the self, which, being subject to constant change in time, is in constant flux and therefore ever outside our grasp—"personality, whose permanent reality can only be apprehended as a retrospective hypothesis. The individual is the seat of a constant process of decantation, sluggish, pale and monochrome, to the vessel containing the fluid of past time, agitated and multicoloured by the phenomena of its hours."

Being subject to this process of time flowing through us and changing us in doing so, we are, at no single moment in our lives, identical with ourselves. Hence "we are disappointed at the nullity of what we are pleased to call attainment. But what is attainment? The identification of the subject with the object of his desire. The subject has died—and perhaps many times on the way." If Godot is the object of Vladimir's and Estragon's desire, he seems naturally ever beyond their reach. It is significant that the boy who acts as go-between fails to recognize the pair from day to day. The French version explicitly states that the boy who appears in the second act is the same boy as the one in the first act, yet the boy denies that he has ever seen the two tramps before and insists that this is the first time he has acted as Godot's messenger. As the boy leaves, Vladimir tries to impress it upon him: "You're sure you saw me, eh, you won't come and tell me tomorrow that you never saw me before?" The boy does not reply, and we know that he will again fail to recognize them. Can we ever be sure that the human beings we meet are the same today as they were yesterday? When Pozzo and Lucky first appear, neither Vladimir nor Estragon seems to recognize them; Estragon even takes Pozzo for Godot. But after they have gone, Vladimir comments that they have changed since their last appearance. Estragon insists that he didn't know them.

> VLADIMIR: Yes you do know them.
> ESTRAGON: No I don't know them.
> VLADIMIR: We know them, I tell you. You forget everything. (*Pause. To himself.*) Unless they're not the same. . . .
> ESTRAGON: Why didn't they recognize us, then?
> VLADIMIR: That means nothing. I too pretended not to recognize them. And then nobody ever recognizes us.

In the second act, when Pozzo and Lucky reappear, cruelly deformed by the action of time, Vladimir and Estragon again have their doubts whether they are the same people they met on the previous day. Nor does Pozzo remember them: "I don't remember having met anyone yesterday. But tomorrow I won't remember having met anyone today."

Waiting is to experience the action of time, which is constant change. And yet, as nothing real ever happens, that change is in itself an illusion. The ceaseless activity of time is self-defeating, purposeless, and therefore null and void. The more things change, the more they are the same. That is the terrible stability of the world. "The tears of the world are a constant quantity. For each one who begins to weep, somewhere else another stops." One day is like another, and when we die, we might never have existed. As Pozzo exclaims in his great final outburst:

> Have you not done tormenting me with your accursed time? . . . One day, is that not enough for you, one day like any other day he went dumb, one day I went blind, one day we'll go deaf, one day we were born, one day we'll die, the same day, the same second. . . . They give birth astride of a grave, the light gleams an instant, then it's night once more.

And Vladimir, shortly afterwards, agrees: "Astride of a grave and a difficult birth. Down in the hole, lingeringly, the gravedigger puts on the forceps."

Still Vladimir and Estragon live in hope: they wait for Godot, whose coming will bring the flow of time to a stop. "Tonight perhaps we shall sleep in his place, in the warmth, dry, our bellies full, on the straw. It is worth waiting for that, is it not?" This passage, omitted in the English version, clearly suggests the peace, the rest from waiting, the sense of having arrived in a haven, that Godot represents to the two tramps. They are hoping to be saved from the evanescence and instability of the illusion of time, and to find peace and permanence outside it. Then they will no longer be tramps, homeless wanderers, but will have arrived home.

Vladimir and Estragon wait for Godot although their appointment with him is by no means certain. Estragon does not remember it at all. Vladimir is not quite sure what they asked Godot to do for them. It was "nothing very definite . . . a kind of prayer . . . a vague supplication." And what had Godot promised them? "That he'd see . . . that he would think it over."

When Beckett is asked about the theme of *Waiting for Godot,* he sometimes refers to a passage in the writings of St Augustine: "There is a wonderful sentence in Augustine. I wish I could remember the Latin. It is even finer in Latin than in English. 'Do not despair: one of the thieves was saved. Do not presume: one of the thieves was damned.' " And Beckett sometimes adds, "I am interested in the shape of ideas even if I do not believe in them. . . . That sentence has a wonderful shape. It is the shape that matters."

The theme of the two thieves on the cross, the theme of the uncertainty of the hope of salvation and the fortuitousness of the bestowal of grace, does indeed pervade the whole play. Vladimir states it right at the beginning: "One of the thieves was saved. . . . It's a reasonable percentage." Later he enlarges on the subject: "Two thieves. . . . One is supposed to have been saved and the other . . . damned. . . . And yet how is it that of the four evangelists only one speaks of a thief being saved? The four of them were there or thereabouts, and only one speaks of a thief being saved. . . . Of the other three two don't mention any thieves at all and the third says that both of them abused him." There is a fifty-fifty chance, but as only one out of four witnesses reports it, the odds are considerably reduced. But, as Vladimir points out; it is a curious fact that everybody seems to believe that one witness: "It is the only version they know." Estragon, whose attitude has been one of scepticism throughout, merely comments, "People are bloody ignorant apes."

It is the shape of the idea that fascinated Beckett. Out of all the malefactors, out of all the millions and millions of criminals that have been executed in the course of history, two, only two, had the chance of receiving absolution in the hour of their death in so uniquely effective a manner. One happened to make a hostile remark; he was damned. One happened to contradict that hostile remark; he was saved. How easily could the roles have been reversed. These, after all, were not well-considered judgements, but chance exclamations uttered at a moment of supreme suffering and stress. As Pozzo says about Lucky, "Remark that I might easily have been in his shoes and he in mine. If chance had not willed it otherwise. To each one his due." And then our shoes might fit us one day and not the next: Estragon's boots torment him in the first act; in act 2 they fit him miraculously.

Godot himself is unpredictable in bestowing kindness and punishment. The boy who is his messenger minds the goats, and Godot treats him well. But the boy's brother, who minds the sheep, is beaten by Godot. "And why doesn't he beat you?" asks Vladimir. "I don't know, sir"—"*Je ne sais pas, Monsieur*"—the boy replies, using the words of the *apache* who had stabbed Beckett. The parallel to Cain and Abel is evident: there too the Lord's grace fell on one rather than on the other without any rational explanation—only that Godot beats the minder of the sheep and cherishes the minder of the goats. Here Godot also acts contrary to the Son of Man at the Last Judgement: "And he shall set the sheep on his right hand, but the goats on the left." But if Godot's kindness is bestowed fortuitously, his coming is not a source of pure joy; it can also mean damnation. When Estragon, in the second act, believes Godot to be approaching, his first thought is, "I'm accursed." And as Vladimir triumphantly exclaims, "It's Godot! At last! Let's go and meet him," Estragon runs away, shouting, "I'm in hell!"

The fortuitous bestowal of grace, which passes human understanding, divides mankind into those that will be saved and those that will be damned. When, in act 2 Pozzo and Lucky return, and the two tramps try to identify them, Estragon calls out, "Abel! Abel!" Pozzo immediately responds. But when Estragon calls out, "Cain! Cain!" Pozzo responds again. "He's all mankind," concludes Estragon.

There is even a suggestion that Pozzo's activity is concerned with his frantic attempt to draw that fifty-fifty chance of salvation upon himself. In the first act, Pozzo is on his way to sell Lucky "at the fair." The French version, however, specifies that it is the *"marché de Saint-Sauveur"*—the Market of the Holy Saviour—to which he is taking Lucky. Is Pozzo trying to sell Lucky to redeem himself? Is he trying to divert the fifty-fifty chance of redemption from Lucky (in whose shoes he might easily have been himself) to Pozzo? He certainly complains that Lucky is causing him great pain, that he is killing him with his mere presence—perhaps because his mere presence reminds Pozzo that it might be Lucky who will be redeemed. When Lucky gives his famous demonstration of his thinking, what is the thin thread of sense that seems to underlie the opening passage of his wild, schizophrenic "word salad"? Again, it seems to be concerned with the fortuitousness of salvation: "Given the existence . . . of a personal God . . . outside time without extension who from the heights of divine apathia divine athambia divine aphasia loves us dearly with some exceptions for reasons unknown . . . and suffers . . . with those who for reasons unknown are plunged in torment." Here again we have the personal God, with his divine apathy, his speechlessness (aphasia), and his lack of the capacity for terror or amazement (athambia), who loves us dearly—with some exceptions, who will be plunged into the torments of hell. In other words, God, who does not communicate with us, cannot feel for us, and condemns us for reasons unknown.

When Pozzo and Lucky reappear the next day, Pozzo blind and Lucky dumb, no more is heard of the fair. Pozzo has failed to sell Lucky; his blindness in thinking that he could thus influence the action of grace has been made evident in concrete physical form.

That *Waiting for Godot* is concerned with the hope of salvation through the workings of grace seems clearly established both from Beckett's own evidence and from the text itself. Does this, however, mean that it is a Christian, or even that it is a religious, play? There have been a number of very ingenious interpretations in this sense. Vladimir's and Estragon's waiting is explained as signifying their steadfast faith and hope, while Vladimir's kindness to his friend, and the two tramps' mutual interdependence, are seen as symbols of Christian charity. But these religious interpretations seem to overlook a number of essential features of the play—its constant stress on the uncertainty of the appointment with Godot, Godot's unreliability and irrationality, and the repeated demonstration of the futility of the hopes pinned on him. The act of waiting for Godot is shown as essentially *absurd*. Admittedly it might be a case of *"Credere quia absurdum est,"* yet it might even more forcibly be taken as a demonstration of the proposition *"Absurdum est credere."*

There is one feature in the play that leads one to assume there is a better solution to the tramps' predicament, which they themselves both consider preferable to waiting for Godot—that is, suicide. "We should have thought of it when the world was young, in the nineties. . . . Hand in hand from the top of the Eiffel Tower, among the first. We were respectable in those days. Now it's too late. They wouldn't even let us up." Suicide remains their favourite solution, unattainable owing to their own incompetence and their lack of the practical tools to achieve it. It is precisely their disappointment at their failure to succeed in their attempts at suicide that Vladimir and Estragon rationalize by waiting, or pretending to wait, for Godot. "I'm curious to hear what he has to offer. Then we'll take it or leave it." Estragon, far less convinced of Godot's promises than Vladimir, is anxious to reassure himself that they are not tied to Godot.

> ESTRAGON: I'm asking you if we are tied.
> VLADIMIR: Tied?
> ESTRAGON: Ti-ed.
> VLADIMIR: How do you mean tied?
> ESTRAGON: Down.
> VLADIMIR: But to whom. By whom?
> ESTRAGON: To your man.
> VLADIMIR: To Godot? Tied to Godot? What an idea! No
>   question of it. (*Pause.*) For the moment.

When, later, Vladimir falls into some sort of complacency about their waiting—"We have kept our appointment . . . we are not saints—but we have kept our appointment. How many people can boast as much?" Estragon immediately punctures it by retorting, "Billions." And Vladimir is quite ready to admit that they are waiting only from irrational habit. "What's certain is that the hours are long . . . and constrain us to beguile them with proceedings . . . which may at first sight seem reasonable until they become a habit. You may say it is to prevent our reason from foundering. No doubt. But has it not long been straying in the night without end of the abyssal depths?"

In support of the Christian interpretation, it might be argued that Vladimir and Estragon, who are waiting for Godot, are shown as clearly superior to Pozzo and Lucky, who have no appointment, no objective, and are wholly egocentric, wholly wrapped up in their sadomasochistic relationship. Is it not their faith that puts the two tramps on to a higher plane?

It is evident that, in fact, Pozzo is naïvely overconfident and self-centred. "Do I look like a man that can be made to suffer?" he boasts. Even when he gives a soulful and melancholy description of the sunset and the sudden falling of the night, we know he does not believe the night will ever fall on him—he is merely giving a performance; he is not concerned with the meaning of what he recites, but only with its effect on the audience. Hence he is taken completely unawares when night does fall on him and he goes blind. Likewise Lucky, in accepting Pozzo as his master and in teaching him his ideas, seems to have been naïvely convinced of the power of reason, beauty, and truth. Estragon and Vladimir *are* clearly superior to both Pozzo and Lucky—not because they pin their faith on Godot but because they are less naïve. They do not believe in action, wealth, or reason. They are aware that all we do in this life is as nothing when seen against the senseless action of time, which is in itself an illusion. They are aware that suicide would be the best solution. They are thus superior to Pozzo and Lucky because they are less self-centred and have fewer illusions. In fact, as a Jungian psychologist, Eva Metman, has pointed out in a remarkable study of Beckett's plays, "Godot's function seems to be to keep his dependents unconscious." In this view, the hope, the habit of hoping, that Godot might come after all is the last illusion that keeps Vladimir and Estragon from facing the human condition and themselves in the harsh light of fully conscious awareness. As Dr Metman observes, it is at the very moment, toward the end of the play, when Vladimir is about to realize he has been dreaming, and must wake up and face the world as it is, that Godot's messenger arrives, rekindles his hopes, and plunges him back into the passivity of illusion.

For a brief moment, Vladimir is aware of the full horror of the human condition: "The air is full of our cries. . . . But habit is a great deadener." He looks at Estragon, who is asleep, and reflects, "At me too someone is looking, of me too someone is saying, he is sleeping, he knows nothing, let him sleep on. . . . I can't go on!" The routine of waiting for Godot stands for habit, which prevents us from reaching the painful but fruitful awareness of the full reality of being.

Again we find Beckett's own commentary on this aspect of *Waiting for Godot* in his essay on Proust: "Habit is the ballast that chains the dog to his vomit. Breathing is habit. Life is habit. Or rather life is a succession of habits, since the individual is a succession of individuals. . . . Habit then is the generic term for the countless treaties concluded between the countless subjects that constitute the individual and their countless correlative objects. The periods of transition that separate consecutive adaptations . . . represent the perilous zones in the life of the individual, dangerous, precarious, painful, mysterious, and fertile, when for a moment the *boredom of living* is replaced by the *suffering of being*." "The suffering of being: that is the free play of every faculty. Because the pernicious devotion of habit paralyses our attention, drugs those handmaidens of perception whose cooperation is not absolutely essential."

Vladimir's and Estragon's pastimes are, as they repeatedly indicate, designed to stop them from thinking. "We're in no danger of thinking any more. . . . Thinking is not the worst. . . . What is terrible is to have thought."

Vladimir and Estragon talk incessantly. Why? They hint at it in what is probably the most lyrical, the most perfectly phrased passage of the play:

> VLADIMIR: You are right, we're inexhaustible.
> ESTRAGON: It's so we won't think.
> VLADIMIR: We have that excuse.
> ESTRAGON: It's so we won't hear.
> VLADIMIR: We have our reasons.
> ESTRAGON: All the dead voices.
> VLADIMIR: They make a noise like wings.
> ESTRAGON: Like leaves.
> VLADIMIR: Like sand.
> ESTRAGON: Like leaves.
>   *Silence.*
> VLADIMIR: They all speak together.
> ESTRAGON: Each one to itself.
>   *Silence.*
> VLADIMIR: Rather they whisper.
> ESTRAGON: They rustle.
> VLADIMIR: They murmur.
> ESTRAGON: They rustle.

Silence.
VLADIMIR: What do they say?
ESTRAGON: They talk about their lives.
VLADIMIR: To have lived is not enough for them.
ESTRAGON: They have to talk about it.
VLADIMIR: To be dead is not enough for them.
ESTRAGON: It is not sufficient.
Silence.
VLADIMIR: They make a noise like feathers.
ESTRAGON: Like leaves.
VLADIMIR: Like ashes.
ESTRAGON: Like leaves.
Long silence.

This passage, in which the cross talk of Irish music-hall comedians is miraculously transmuted into poetry, contains the key to much of Beckett's work. Surely these rustling, murmuring voices of the past are the voices we hear in the three novels of his trilogy; they are the voices that explore the mysteries of being and the self to the limits of anguish and suffering. Vladimir and Estragon are trying to escape hearing them. The long silence that follows their evocation is broken by Vladimir, *"in anguish,"* with the cry "Say anything at all!" after which the two relapse into their wait for Godot.

The hope of salvation may be merely an evasion of the suffering and anguish that spring from facing the reality of the human condition. There is here a truly astonishing parallel between the existentialist philosophy of Jean-Paul Sartre and the creative intuition of Beckett, who has never consciously expressed existentialist views. If, for Beckett as for Sartre, man has the duty of facing the human condition as a recognition that at the root of our being there is nothingness, liberty, and the need of constantly creating ourselves in a succession of choices, then Godot might well become an image of what Sartre calls "bad faith"—"The first act of bad faith consists in evading what one cannot evade, in evading what one *is.*"

While these parallels may be illuminating, we must not go too far in trying to identify Beckett's vision with any school of philosophy. It is the peculiar richness of a play like *Waiting for Godot* that it opens vistas on so many different perspectives. It is open to philosophical, religious, and psychological interpretations, yet above all it is a poem on time, evanescence, and the mysteriousness of existence, the paradox of change and stability, necessity and absurdity. It expresses what Watt felt about the household of Mr Knott: "nothing changed in Mr Knott's establishment, because nothing remained, and nothing came or went, because all was a coming and a going." In watching *Waiting for Godot,* we feel like Watt contemplating the organization of Mr Knott's world: "But he had hardly felt the absurdity of those things, on the one hand, and the necessity of those others, on the other, (for it is rare that the feeling of absurdity is not followed by the feeling of necessity), when he felt the absurdity of those things of which he had just felt the necessity (for it is rare that the feeling of necessity is not followed by the feeling of absurdity)."

Waiting

Ruby Cohn

How describe its initial impact to a generation that has grown up with *Godot*? Now that any serious drama seeks a mythic dimension; now that disjunction is the familiar rhetorical pattern of stage speech; now that tragic depth almost always wears clown costume; now that the gestures of drama border on dance; now that expositions are quainter than soliloquies, and stage presence implies neither past nor future—now it may be hard to recall that it was not always so. *En attendant Godot* brought the curtain down on King Ibsen.

After nearly two decades, my bad memory clings to the warmth of that first *Godot* on a damp winter night. I had never heard of Beckett when I first saw *Godot*. I did not know my Bible well enough to recognize the scriptural kernel of the play. I had not read Hegel's *Phenomenology of Mind* well enough to recognize the archetypical master–slave relationship. I was not even a devotee of silent comic films. In short, I came to *Godot* with no background; or with too much background of Broadway problem plays, Comédie Française classics, and verse drama wherever I could find it. And yet I knew almost at once that those two French-speaking tramps were me; more miserable, more lovable, more humorous, more desperate. But me.

Laughter did not ring out through the little Théâtre de Babylone, as in performances I saw later. Rather, chuckles faded into smiles or frowns. I must have been too full of feeling to notice the unusual stage silences through which I fidgeted in later productions. The élan

From *Back to Beckett*. © 1973 by Princeton University Press.

of those aboriginal Beckett tramps carried me right over the silences. But Pozzo and Lucky repelled me, recalling a circus-master and his trained animal. Long a coward about physical pain, I could hardly look at Lucky's neck, for fear of seeing his bruises, and I looked with distaste at Pozzo who supposedly caused the bruises I didn't see. Lucky's monologue was so terrible to watch, with Jean Martin's spastic tics, that I thought *that* was the reason I could make no sense of it. I was ashamedly relieved when the other three characters shut Lucky up, and I was not sorry to see what I thought would be the last of him and his master. I can recall none of my intermission questions, but I can still see the act 2 leaves on the tree, like shreds of green crepe paper. And I caught the point of the dog-song at once. "That's what the play is about," I must have told myself, as I settled back familiarly into the patter of the two tramps. I was surprised by the return of Pozzo and Lucky, no more sympathetic when maimed and subdued. I was even more surprised at the callousness with which the friends treated the unfortunate couple. But I wasn't surprised that Godot didn't come. I was pretty sure that the end of the play *was* the end, but I was pleased to have this confirmed by scattered applause, in which I joined vigorously. I can't remember the number of curtain calls, but there weren't many.

How was *Godot* received by other audiences who did not know that it was to become a classic? It was a running gag in Miami, the American opening city, that taxis could be sure of fares at the end of act 1. Michael Myerberg advertised for (and did not find) an audience of 80,000 intellectuals in New York City. Moving response came from San Quentin prison, but Herbert Blau nearly had a mutiny in his company before he persuaded them to do the play that was so meaningful for prisoners. Several of its first directors returned for another round with *Godot*—Blin, Blau, Schneider. In 1966 Yugoslavian Miodrag Bulatović wrote a sequel, *Godot Came*. Before the death of Bertold Brecht in 1956, he wanted to adapt Beckett's play, and in 1971 Peter Palitsch, once Brecht's student, produced a Brechtian *Godot*, replete with gestus and estrangement. Though the original reception of *Godot* was unexpectedly good, enthusiasm for it is still far from universal. In 1956 Bert Lahr-Gogo received a letter denouncing the play as "communistic, atheistic, and existential." In May 1971, an American college professor was forced to resign after directing *Godot*, which was declared "detrimental to the moral fibre of the college community."

Beckett would be the last to defend *Godot*. "I began to write *Godot*," he told Colin Duckworth, "as a relaxation, to get away from the awful prose I was writing at that time." I have tried to show that if the prose of the trilogy is awful, it is in the sense of awe-inspiring, and yet I can guess at what Beckett meant. Malone was unable to stick to his spirit of system; doubt eroded each scene he tried to present. The Unnamable was waiting in the wings or the cellarage. In turning to dramatic form, Beckett may have been seeking an order that he could not honestly impose on his fiction. Later he was to tell Michael Haerdter: "That's the value of theater for me. You place on stage a little world with its own laws." But Beckett's little stage worlds are emblematic of our big real world.

The seed of *Godot* is Luke's account of the crucifixion, as summarized by St. Augustine: "Do not despair: one of the thieves was saved. Do not presume: one of the thieves was damned." The two thieves are Didi and Gogo; the two thieves are Pozzo and Lucky; the two thieves are you and me. And the play is shaped to reflect that fearful symmetry. I am not for a moment suggesting that this was a conscious choice on Beckett's part. Embroiled as he was in the murky lyricism of the trilogy, he sought the repose of order—"cawm," as Gogo would say. The *Godot* manuscript bears evidence of Beckett's sure shaping touch; the handwriting, unusually legible rather than cramped with effort, flows along with few changes. The dialogue rhythm, as Colin Duckworth has shown in careful detail, leans on that of *Mercier et Camier,* but the basic form comes from St. Augustine.

Even before the curtain rises, the program informs us that there will be *two* acts, though we do not know how the second will reflect the first. The set pits the horizontal road on the stage board against the vertical tree. The action will balance four characters falling *down* against their looking *up* at the sky. The very names of the four main characters indicate their pairing: Pozzo and Lucky contain two syllables and five letters each; Estragon and Vladimir contain three syllables and eight letters each, but they address one another only by nicknames—Gogo and Didi, childish four-letter words composed of repeated monosyllables. Even the fifth character, the nameless boy, has a brother, and he says that Godot beats the one but not the other. Godot is as arbitrary as the God of Matthew 25:32–33: "And before him shall be gathered all nations: and he shall separate them one from another, as a shepherd divideth his sheep from the goats. And he shall set the sheep on his right hand but the goats on the left." Sheep and goat become saved thief and damned thief of St. Augustine's symmetry.

Didi broods about the two thieves early in the play, as we are getting acquainted with what look like two thieves on stage. Though it is not specified in the text, Beckett's two thieves wear similar clothes in production—the black suit and derby of music hall or silent film, and we laugh at their antics much of the time that they are constantly before us. (For Roger Blin, the ideal cast would have been Chaplin as Didi, Keaton as Gogo, and Laughton as Pozzo.) Pozzo and Lucky have no nicknames, and we view them formally, externally, during their intermittent presence before us. Their clothes are elaborate but dated, their relationship is repulsive, but it is not really our business. Pozzo seems to want to become our business (through the friends), lush as he is with self-revelation (to the friends), but he himself warns that "there wasn't a word of truth in it." Lucky speaks of his civilization rather than himself in his single long monologue, which contains the word "I" only in the mechanical phrase, "I resume." Impersonal Pozzo and Lucky confront personal Gogo and Didi, and for all the many pages that have now been written about the play, *Godot*'s theatricality rests very squarely on this confrontation of two couples. To twist what Beckett said about the two-act structure of *Godot*: one couple would have been too few, and three would have been too many. Pozzo and Lucky alone would have been a caricature of human master-slave tendencies, a caricature of human obsession with moving "On." Caricatures summon no sympathy. Without these contrasting caricatures, however, we would respond less immediately to the concreteness of Didi and Gogo. We appreciate their friendship in the contrapuntal context of Pozzo and Lucky. In the shadow of these compulsive wanderers, who wander into obvious deterioration, Didi and Gogo scintillate with variety. Each couple is more meaningful because of the other, replacing the protagonist and antagonist of dramatic tradition.

None of these symmetries is exact, of course. Act 2 does not repeat act 1 precisely. Each member of each couple is distinctive and individual. And looming asymmetrically offstage is Godot. The very first review suggested that Godot might be "happiness, eternal life, the unattainable quest of all men." And Godot has subsequently been explained as God, a diminutive god, Love, Death, Silence, Hope, De Gaulle, Pozzo, a Balzac character, a bicycle racer, Time Future, a

Paris street for call girls, a distasteful image evoked by French words containing the root *god* (*godailler*, to guzzle; *godenot*, runt; *godelureau*, bumpkin; *godichon*, lout). Beckett told Roger Blin that the name Godot derived from French slang words for boot—*godillot, godasse*. A decade after *Godot* was produced, I informed Beckett of a San Francisco mortician's firm, Godeau Inc. Beckett's play tells us plainly who Godot is—the promise that is always awaited and not fulfilled, the expectation that brings two men to the board night after night. The play tells us this dramatically and not discursively.

St. Augustine commented on the crucifixions in Luke's gospel: "Do not despair: one of the thieves was saved. Do not presume: one of the thieves was damned." Fifty percent may be a reasonable chance, but only one of the four gospels argues for that percentage, so that Didi arrives at a dimmer view: "But all four were there. And only one speaks of a thief being saved." It is no wonder then that Didi and Gogo are more tempted to despair than to presume. And yet they do not despair. Instead, they keep their appointment, and they wait. Night after night, they keep their appointment, and they wait. While they wait, they repeat the activities that add up to a life.

From the beginning of the play Didi and Gogo emphasize the repetitive nature of their activities. Were Beckett to direct the play, he would now begin with their attitude of waiting, which would be periodically repeated throughout the play. In the printed text the play begins when Estragon tries *again* to take off his boots. We read the first example of a frequently repeated scenic direction: *"As before"* (in French, even more pointedly, *"Même jeu,"* literally *"Same play"*). In Vladimir's first speech he talks about *resuming* the struggle. He notes that Estragon is there *again*—wherever "there" may be. He is glad that Estragon is *back*—wherever "back" may be. Vladimir wants to celebrate his *reunion* with Estragon.

In the first few minutes of playing time each of the friends asks the significant question: "It hurts?" And the other answers: "Hurts! He wants to know if it hurts!" This first of the many repetitions of the dialogue makes pain general, but also musical. Beckett never sacrifices meaning to sound, but as in his complex fiction he often intensifies meaning through sound.

Immediately after the first utterance of the most frequently repeated line in the play—"We're waiting for Godot"—the friends turn their attention to the stage tree. Estragon says: "Looks to me more like a bush." Vladimir counters: "A shrub." But Estragon insists: "A bush." This exchange sets a pattern of poetic variants and refrains, with Estragon always speaking the refrain lines. Throughout the play, phrasal repetition, most naked in Lucky's manic monologue, is reinforced by gestural repetition: Lucky with his luggage, Pozzo with his possessions, Gogo with his shoes, Didi with his hat, and the music-hall routine in which Gogo and Didi juggle three hats (suggested to Beckett by the Marx Brothers' *Duck Soup*). All the characters repeatedly stumble and fall, but in act 1 Didi and Gogo set Lucky on his feet, and in act 2 they do the same for Pozzo. Repetition is theme and technique of Didi's round-song which reduces man's life to a dog's life—and cruel death.

In the printed text of *En attendant Godot* the most frequent repetitions are two scenic directions: *Silence* and *Pause*. In the theater repeated stillness can reach a point of no return, but Beckett avoids this danger by adroit deployment of his pauses and silences. They act like theatrical punctuation, a pause often marking hesitation or qualification, whereas silence is a brush with despair before making a fresh start. The play never quite negates a fresh start after stillness claims the stage in sudden night. All stage action has to be wrested from the background stillness, the ever-threatening void. Gogo realizes: "There's no lack of void." And he recalls talking about "*nothing* in particular." (The italics are mine; Beckett changes the French "boots" to "nothing" in the English version.) Each of the two acts ends with the stillness after the same lines: "Well? Shall we go?" asks one of the friends, and the other replies: "Yes, let's go." In neither act do they move as the curtain falls.

The opening "Nothing to be done" is repeated three times. What distinguishes drama from fiction is that the Nothing has to be done, acted, performed. The body of Beckett's play therefore contains much doing, constantly threatened by Nothing. To open each act, Gogo and Didi enter separately, each in turn first on stage. At least one of them eats, excretes, sleeps, dreams, remembers, plans, refers to sex or suicide. In both acts they comment on their reunion, they complain of their misery, they seek escape into games, they are frightened by offstage menace, they try to remember a past, they stammer a hope for a future, they utter doubts about time, place, and language, they wait for Godot. Beckett's scenic directions show the range of their emotions: irritably, coldly, admiringly, decisively, gloomily, cheerfully, feebly, angrily, musingly, despairingly, very insidiously, looking wildly about, wheedling, voluptuously, gently, highly excited, grotesquely rigid, violently, meditatively, vacuously, timidly, conciliating, hastily, grudgingly, stutteringly, resolute, vehemently, forcibly, tenderly, blankly, indignantly, attentively, sadly, shocked, joyous, indifferent, vexed, suddenly furious, exasperated, sententious, in anguish, sure of himself, controlling himself, triumphantly, stupefied, softly, recoiling, alarmed, laughing noisily, sagging, painfully, feverishly—with violently and despairingly most frequent.

In each act the two friends are diverted by an interlude—the play within the play of Pozzo and Lucky, who enter and exit tied together. Reciting rhetorically and loaded with props, Pozzo and Lucky are cut down to size when they are "done" by Gogo and Didi in act 2. Alone again in each act, the friends are greeted by Godot's messenger, they hear the monotonous message, and the moon rises swiftly. Refrains, repetitions, and pauses camouflage how *much* is happening on stage. Only in retrospect, after viewing it all, do we realize how much is at stake in these hapless happenings.

V. A. Kolve has compared *Godot* to medieval drama: in the Corpus Christi plays, Holy Saturday, the day between Christ's death and resurrection, is the day when nothing can be known or done, when faith is eroded by doubt. Didi and Gogo are to meet Godot on Saturday, but no Easter dawns with its promise of resurrection. The other medieval form, the morality play, portrays Everyman seeking salvation, the medieval human condition. But conditions have changed since the Middle Ages. Didi ponders salvation, but he has to rack his brain before he can think of the opposite of salvation: the damnation that must have been vividly present in the medieval mind, but that is modern everyday reality. Modern man knows no psychomachia; he waits out a life of Holy Saturdays, closer to the passivity of Zen than to redemption. "Doing the tree" of *Godot* is exercise 52 in the yoga series, standing on one leg to pray, but Gogo cannot keep his balance, and there is no evidence that God sees him.

While waiting for Godot, Didi and Gogo act out their condition, together and alone. Gogo, as his name suggests (English "go"), is the more physical in his needs, complaints, perceptions. Didi, as his name suggests (French "dis"), is more voluble and philosophical. They are interdependent, and yet each is a whole man and not an allegorical abstraction. Simply human, each of them suffers while waiting, but they react against suffering by trying to fill or kill the time of waiting. Their activities have an improvisational quality—

dancing, juggling, tumbling, miming, falling, and rising—with Gogo the more active of the two. Their dialogue is varied with questions and exclamations, logic and disjunction, incompleteness and alternatives, erudition and obscenity, synonyms and antonyms, paradox and incongruity, tenderness and imprecation—with Didi the more inventive of the two. Their first discussion of Godot is a music-hall routine, and their duet about dead voices is, in Herbert Blau's phrase, "a superb threnody on desire, mortality, and time." Physically and metaphysically, their words and gestures penetrate our own.

Most of us, however, would be reluctant to see ourselves in the doings of Pozzo and Lucky. Pozzo and Lucky of act 1 are ready performers, and their flagrant contrast is part of the performance. They dress according to their social station; Pozzo flourishes his props (whip, pipe, atomizer, watch) whereas Lucky bends under burdens. Lucky can dance and think; actor Jack MacGowran has indicated the three threads of Lucky's monologue: the constancy of the divine, the shrinkage of humanity, the petrifaction of the earth. Lucky's monologue displays Western civilization as shards of religion, philosophy, science, art, sport, and modern industry. In that monologue, Lucky utters the word "unfinished" seven times; his sentences do not finish, and his monologue is not permitted to finish. Named with devastating irony, Lucky is modern man with his contradictory unfinished fragments.

The Pozzo of act 1 needs all eyes on him to answer a simple question. He recites an elocution piece with studied gestures. But though he may be a dilettante, he has meditated on time and life, theory and practice. Physically, he and Lucky lack the friends' gestural variety, and yet they do move about. Lucky carries, and Pozzo sits; both of them fall and shakily rise. Compulsively, they voyage "on," perhaps to perform at another encounter. Both master and servant deliver set pieces of dialogue, too thoroughly rehearsed. Pozzo resembles a disc jockey or television announcer, and Lucky a broken record. But by act 2, Lucky is dumb, and blind Pozzo speaks only in passion. No longer able to entertain, they present their misery for the friends' diversion. When Didi questions Pozzo, as a journalist might question yesterday's star actor, Pozzo explodes into the most haunting line of the play: "They give birth astride of a grave, the light gleams an instant, then it's night once more." The night is immeasurably more profound than the twilight of Pozzo's act 1 set piece.

Though less obstreperous than Pozzo and Lucky, Didi and Gogo are also performers. Gogo is a would-be raconteur, and Didi paraphrases the Bible. In act 1 Pozzo and perhaps Lucky are aware of being performers, but Didi and perhaps Gogo are aware of being in a play. And they are aware of playing to pass time: "We always find something, eh Didi, to give us the impression we exist?" In giving us that intense impression, the two friends undercut their mockery of their own play. "We are bored to death," complains Didi. Millions of spectators have been entertained by that boredom.

One of the most time-conscious plays ever written, *En attendant Godot* has itself been buffeted by time. In 1971, the same year that it was said to undermine the moral fibre of a college community, *Time* magazine's reporter took a deep breath and pronounced it "no masterpiece" for much the same reason: "*Waiting for Godot* is Beckett's tomb. Need it necessarily be ours?" We seem to have come full circle to some of the early Sunday-supplement reaction to *Godot*. And it is not uncheering that, in spite of the reams that have been written about *Godot,* it can still disturb.

Beyond a very few references, I have said little about these reams. The first book about Beckett focuses largely on *Godot,* and every year brings new interpretations. I have edited a volume that contains theatrical, source, genre, Marxist, Christian, mythic, philosophic, phenomenological, imagistic, linguistic interpretations of *Godot.* Other editors have included other approaches. Many discussions are illuminating, but none is indispensable. It is not even indispensable, or especially helpful, to know Beckett's other works in order to respond to *Godot.* I do not believe that *Godot* is Beckett's greatest work, but it is perhaps his most immediate. As *Malone* presents us with the building blocks of stories, *Godot* shows us how hard it is to build a play. And since playing is the most direct imitation of living, theater can evoke the most immediate audience response.

I lingered so long on my own first reaction to *Godot* because it is hard today to see *Godot* without ever having heard of it. But if one could, I think one would—as I did—virtually build the play along with the actors. Not in amateur admixtures *à la* "happening," but through absorption in Beckett's scenes. Unlike previous drama that posits a past, *Godot*'s *thereness* unrolls before our perceptions, as Alain Robbe-Grillet understood so early. Only the opening lines are gratuitous in *Godot.* After that each line is uttered on cue. Nor does such sequence contradict what I said earlier about the drama's improvisational quality. Improvisation, as today's actors well know, is hard work. Improvisation is not synonymous with spontaneous effervescence. Stage time has to be played through, and each line, each gesture, takes effort. Combining lines and gestures may result from tedious rehearsal, as in Pozzo's set piece; or word and motion may remain separate. Even words demanding motion may not attain it. Estragon says "Over there" without gesture. When he says, "I'm going," he goes nowhere. Vladimir offers to give Lucky a handkerchief, but he does not approach him. And each act's curtain-line is, "Yes, let's go," but the two actors *"do not move."*

All this serves to focus attention on the very elements of drama—entrances, exits, silence, cues, repartee, blocking, and the offstage unknown. Least subtle in *Godot* are the lines that refer to the play as a play: "This is becoming really insignificant." "I've been better entertained." However, the lines embrace more than the particular situation. And it is this extensibility, rooted in particulars, that ultimately makes a classic of *Godot,* as of *Hamlet.* Hamlet's questions—specific questions in the play's dialogue—probe to a depth undreamed of in our revenge plays. *Godot*'s questions—questions, often unanswered, constitute about one quarter of the play's sentences—probe to a metaphysics undreamed of in our physics. The play's opening assertion, "Nothing to be done" (even more casual in the French cliché *"Rien à faire"),* is spoken by Estragon about his boots. But Vladimir picks it up as a metaphysical generalization: "I'm beginning to come round to that opinion. All my life I've tried to put it from me." By the end of the play, Vladimir is still living, so he is still trying to put it from him, still only coming round to that opinion. During the course of the play, he has made such metaphysical observations as: "Where are all these corpses from?" "There's no lack of void." "Time has stopped." "But at this place at this moment of time, all mankind is us, whether we like it or not." (The cross-nationality of the names of the four characters reinforces this assertion.) More humorously, Estragon utters comparably cosmic lines: "People are bloody ignorant apes." "Pah! The wind in the reeds" (on a dusty highway). "Everything oozes." "I'm tired breathing." Near the end, Vladimir paraphrases Pozzo's heartrending line: "Astride of a grave and a difficult birth. Down in the hole, lingeringly, the grave digger puts on the forceps.

We have time to grow old. The air is full of our cries." Like other single speeches in the tragicomedy, *that* is what *Godot* is about. "Our cries" compose its dialogue, orchestrated by Beckett, and understood in many languages.

*W*aiting for Godot

Hugh Kenner

Robinson Crusoe, a romance about one man rebuilding the world, becomes a different kind of book when his island proves to contain a second man, black Friday. A *pair* of men has an irreducibly primitive appeal. They can talk to one another, and it soon becomes clear how little either one is capable of saying. Each is "a little world made cunningly," each has enjoyed many many thousands of hours of the fullest consciousness of which he is capable, each has learned to speak, and learned to cipher, and seen perhaps many cities like Odysseus, or perhaps just Manchester. Each has been torn by passions, each has known calm, each has ingested a universe through his five senses, and arranged its elements in his mind for ready access according to social and pedagogical custom. And they can share almost none of all this. Toward one another they turn faces that might almost as well be blank spheres, and wonderful as words are they can speak, each of them, but one word at a time, so that they must arrange these words in strings, poor starved arrangements, virtually empty by comparison with all that presses within them to be said.

On the first page of his last novel, *Bouvard et Pécuchet,* Flaubert in his fierce drive after essentials described an empty street like an empty stage; caused two men to enter this place from opposite sides and sit down simultaneously on the same bench; saw to it that the day should be so hot they would remove their hats to wipe their

From *A Reader's Guide to Samuel Beckett.* © 1973 by Thames and Hudson Ltd. Farrar, Straus & Giroux, 1973.

brows; and had each, naturally, set his hat down on the bench.

> And the smaller man saw written in his neighbour's hat, "Bouvard," while the latter easily made out in the cap of the individual wearing the frock-coat the word "Pécuchet."
> "Fancy that," he said. "We've both had the idea of writing our names in our hats."
> "Good heavens, yes; mine might be taken at the office."
> "The same with me; I work in an office too."

So begins the mutual disclosure of two mortals, two immortal souls; and what they have to disclose, though lifetimes would not suffice, is somehow packed into the hemispherical spaces those hats were made to enclose.

Beckett's immediate model for the pair of men in *Waiting for Godot* would seem to be less literary than this. Didi and Gogo in their bowler hats, one of them marvellously incompetent, the other an ineffective man of the world devoted (some of the time) to his friend's care, resemble nothing so much as they do the classic couple of 1930s cinema, Stan Laurel and Oliver Hardy, whose troubles with such things as hats and boots were notorious, and whose dialogue was spoken very slowly on the assumption that the human understanding could not be relied on to work at lightning speed. The *mise-en-scène* of their films was a country of dreams, at least in this respect, that no explanation of their relationship was ever ventured. They journeyed, they undertook quests, they had adventures; their friendship, tested by bouts of exasperation, was never really vulnerable; they seemed not to become older, nor wiser; and in perpetual nervous agitation, Laurel's nerves occasionally protesting like a baby's, Hardy soliciting a philosophic calm he could never quite find leisure to settle into, they coped. Neither was especially competent, but Hardy made a big man's show of competence. Laurel was defeated by the most trifling requirements. Hence, in *Way Out West* (1937):

> HARDY: Get on the mule.
> LAUREL: What?
> HARDY: Get *on* the mule.

which comes as close as we need ask to the exchange in the last moments of *Godot*:

> VLADIMIR: Pull on your trousers.
> ESTRAGON: What?

> VLADIMIR: Pull on your trousers.
> ESTRAGON: You want me to pull off my trousers?
> VLADIMIR: Pull ON your trousers.
> ESTRAGON: (*realizing his trousers are down*). True.
> *He pulls up his trousers.*

In the same film there is much fuss with Laurel's boots, the holes in which he patches with inedible meat, thus attracting unwanted dogs. *Waiting for Godot* begins:

> *Estragon, sitting on a low mound, is trying to take off his boot. He pulls at it with both hands, panting. He gives up, exhausted, rests, tries again. As before. Enter Vladimir.*
> ESTRAGON: (*giving up again*). Nothing to be done.

Insofar as the play has a "message," that is more or less what it is: "Nothing to be done." There is no dilly-dallying; it is delivered in the first moments, with the first spoken words, as though to get the didactic part out of the way. And yet they go on *doing,* if we are to call it doing. There is a ritual exchange of amenities, from which we learn that Vladimir (as it were, Hardy) takes pride in his superior savoir-faire ("When I think of it . . . all those years . . . but for me . . . where would you be . . . [*Decisively.*] You'd be nothing more than a little heap of bones at the present minute, no doubt about it"). We also learn that if Estragon has chronic foot trouble, Vladimir has chronic bladder trouble. The dialogue comes round again to the theme words "Nothing to be done," this time spoken by Vladimir; and as he speaks these words the action also comes round to where it started, with Estragon by a supreme effort belying the words and pulling off his boot. That is one thing accomplished anyhow.

> *He peers inside it, feels about inside it, turns it upside down, shakes it, looks on the ground to see if anything has fallen out, finds nothing, feels inside it again, staring sightlessly before him.*

These are instructions to an actor, though few actors succeed in finding out how to follow them. It is just here that many productions begin to go astray, the actor supposing that he is called upon to enact something cosmic. Either that, or he patters through the gestures mindlessly, in a hurry to get to something he can make sense of. His best recourse would be to imagine how Stan Laurel would inspect the interior of a boot, intent as though an elephant might drop out of it, or some other key to life's problems.

We have here a problem of style, to be confronted before we proceed. There is something misleading about this printed text, and yet the perusal of the printed text is one of the only two ways of encountering *Waiting for Godot,* the other being at a performance that may have gone totally wrong because of the way the actors and the director responded to the printed text. And yet the printed text is the score for a performance, and is not meant in any final way for reading matter. Therefore we had better be *imagining* a performance at least. This means imagining men speaking the words, instead of ourselves simply reading over the words. The words are not statements the author makes to us, the words are exchanged. "Nothing to be done" is apt to sit on the printed page like the dictum of an oracle. "Nothing to be done," addressed by Estragon (*"giving up again"*) to the problem of removing his boot, is a different matter. It expresses his sense of helplessness with respect to a specific task. There may be, in other contexts, something to be done, though he is not at the moment prepared to envisage them.

But we are in a play, and not in the great world that abounds in "other contexts," and must wait for such contexts as the play chooses to afford in its own good time. Much as Laurel and Hardy must be understood to exist only within that strange universe the Laurel and Hardy film, so the actors exist inside the universe of this play. If that universe should prove to contain only two themes, the need to take off a boot and the impossibility of doing it, the nature of dramatic universes would not be contradicted. Esteemed plays have been built out of elements scarcely more numerous, for instance the obligation to keep Agamemnon from being killed, and the impossibility of this.

The actors exist inside the universe of the play. But—here is a further nuance—they are live actors, living people whose feet resound on floorboards, whose chests move as they breathe, and we must learn to understand, with a corner of our attention, that they are *imprisoned* inside this play. They are people with opinions and digestions, but their freedom tonight is restricted. They are not at liberty to speak any words but the words set down for them, which are not inspiriting words. (In another Beckett play one actor's question, "What is there to keep me here?" is unanswerably answered by the other actor: "The dialogue.") This is always true in plays, as generally in films: it is by following a script that the actors give us the illusion that they are free, and if an actor forgets his lines we discern from his stricken face how little free he is to improvise.

So it is up to the actor to take very seriously the world of the play, which is the only world (and the only play) he is understood to know; and if in the world of the play he is instructed to examine the interior of his boot, why, let him not think of "meaning" but let him examine it. There is nothing else to be done.

"Sam," asked an actor at a rehearsal of *Endgame,* "How do I say to Hamm, 'If I knew the combination of the safe, I'd kill you?' " And Sam Beckett answered quietly, "Just think that if you knew the combination of the safe, you would kill him."

This play's world contains more than Vladimir and Estragon. Before the pair have been on stage three minutes, we learn of the existence of some folk called "they," who administer beatings. Estragon says he spent the night in a ditch, "over there," and on being asked if they didn't beat him, responds that certainly they beat him. The same lot as usual? He doesn't know. "They" and their beatings need no explanation; as much as the sunrise, they are part of this world. The Eiffel Tower, though not hereabouts, is also part of this world, with custodians so fastidious they wouldn't let our pair enter the elevator. Things were not always so. The two before us were once themselves fastidious. Back in those days ("a million years ago, in the nineties") they might have had the sense to lose heart, and gone "hand in hand from the top of the Eiffel Tower, among the first." It is too late now.

What else is part of this world? Memories of the Bible, a proper Protestant Bible with coloured maps at the back. The need to fill up time with conversation ("Come on, Gogo, return the ball, can't you, once in a way?"). Utter impoverishment of local amenities (the only thing to look at is not much of a tree, so nondescript it is perhaps a shrub). And an obligation:

> Let's go.
> We can't.
> Why not?
> We're waiting for Godot.
> (*despairingly*) Ah!

He is said to have said we were to wait by the tree, if this is the tree he meant, and if this is the day.

He didn't say for sure he'd come.
And if he doesn't come?
We'll come back tomorrow.
And then the day after tomorrow.
Possibly.
And so on.

"Godot," let it be stipulated, is pronounced Go-*dough,* accent on the second syllable. The play moreover was written and for some time performed only in French, so it seems largely an accident of the English language that has caused so many readers (some of whom say "*God*-oh") to be distracted by the bit of dialogue that speaks of "a kind of prayer" and "a vague supplication" some moments after mention of Godot. It is simpler by far to stay inside the play, and dismiss interpretations. Godot, inside the play, is the mysterious one for whom we wait. It is not clear why we wait, except that we said we would, and there are hints that he has it in his power to make a difference. "Let's wait till we know exactly how we stand."

Once upon a time, it is worth recalling, there was an audience for this play not a man of whom knew that Godot would never come. It would be nearly impossible to recruit such an audience now, or even such a reader, much as it would be impossible to find a reader for whom there really exists the open possibility that Hamlet will take revenge and then marry Ophelia. Everyone knows that this is the Play about Waiting for the Man Who Doesn't Come, and it is curious how little difference this knowledge makes. If, to the hypothetical innocent viewer, Godot's coming is an open possibility, still he is not encouraged to expect Godot, or to expect anything of him. The play constructs about its two actors the conditions and the quality of waiting, so much so that no one blames the dramatist's perverse whim for the withholding of Godot and the disappointment of their expectations.

Someone however does come: Pozzo comes. He makes so theatrical an entrance that Estragon easily supposes he is Godot. Of course Estragon is impressionable, but apparently Vladimir supposes it as well, though he quickly denies that any such thought crossed his mind. ("You took me for Godot." "Oh no, Sir, not for an instant, Sir.") From this exchange, and from Pozzo's stern interrogation ("Who is he?" and "Waiting? So you were waiting for him?") and from their hasty disavowals ("We hardly know him" and "Personally I wouldn't know him even if I saw him") we gather that the world of the play is one in which it is prudent to know as little as possible. And Pozzo, for all his habit of command, appears to be in flight across the blasted landscape, his servant loaded with what may be loot but is more likely salvage: a heavy bag, a folding stool, a picnic basket, a greatcoat. The rope that joins them, the whip with which Pozzo threatens, are symbols of authority, indispensible because custom, the normal bond of authority, seems to have broken down.

Very well. Two men waiting, for another whom they know only by an implausible name which may not be his real name. A ravaged and blasted landscape. A world that was ampler and more open once, but is permeated with pointlessness now. Mysterious dispensers of beatings. A man of property and his servant, in flight. And the anxiety of the two who wait, their anxiety to be as inconspicuous as possible in a strange environment ("We're not from these parts, Sir") where their mere presence is likely to cause remark. It is curious how readers and audiences do not think to observe the most obvious thing about the world of this play, that it resembles France occupied by the Germans, in which its author spent the war years. How much waiting must have gone on in that bleak world; how many times must Resistance operatives—displaced persons when everyone was displaced, anonymous ordinary people for whom every day renewed the dispersal of meaning—have kept appointments not knowing whom they were to meet, with men who did not show up and may have had good reasons for not showing up, or bad, or may even have been taken; how often must life itself not have turned on the skill with which overconspicuous strangers did nothing as inconspicuously as possible, awaiting a rendezvous, put off by perhaps unreliable messengers, and making do with quotidian ignorance in the principal working convention of the Resistance, which was to let no one know any more than he had to.

We can easily see why a Pozzo would be unnerving. His every gesture is Prussian. He may be a Gestapo official clumsily disguised.

Here is perhaps the playwright's most remarkable feat. There existed, throughout a whole country for five years, a literal situation that corresponded point by point with the situation in this play, and was so far from special that millions of lives were saturated in its desperate reagents, and no spectator ever thinks of it. Instead the play is ascribed to one man's gloomy view of life, which is like crediting him with having invented a good deal of modern history. Not that modern history, nor the Occupation, is the "key" to the play, its solution; it is simply, if we do happen to think of it, a validation of the play. And Beckett saw the need of keeping thoughts of the Occupation from being too accessible, because of the necessity to keep the play from being "about" an event that time has long since absorbed. Sean O'Casey's plays, being "about" the Irish troubles, slide rapidly into the past, period pieces like the photographs in old magazines. *Waiting for Godot* in the 1970s is little changed from what it was the day it was first performed in 1953, a play about a mysterious world where two men wait. We may state its universality in this way: only a fraction of the human race experienced the German occupation of France, and only a fraction of that fraction waited, on Resistance business, for some Godot. But everyone, everywhere, has waited, and wondered why he waited.

There were plays, once, about the House of Atreus, which touched on the racial genealogy of the spectators, and on the origins of customs vivid to them daily. Such plays hold interest today only thanks to the work of time, which has greatly modified them. What seemed fact once seems made up now, part of the set of conventions we must learn and absorb, and the dramatic doings—Agamemnon's murder, Cassandra's rant—have acquired the authority of powerful abstractions. The effort of Beckett's play in suppressing specific reference, in denying itself for example the easy recourse of alarming audiences with references to the Gestapo, would seem to be like an effort to arrive directly at the result of time's work: to perform, while the play is still in its pristine script, the act of abstraction which change and human forgetfulness normally perform, and so to arouse not indignation and horror but more settled emotions. We seem to be a long way from Laurel and Hardy, but the formula of the play was to move the world of the Occupation into Laurel and Hardy's theatre, where it becomes something rich and strange, as do they.

So the play is not "about"; it is itself; it is a play. This sounds impossibly arty unless we reflect that *Hamlet,* for instance, is not about dynastic irregularities in Denmark, a subject in which no Dane could now beat up an interest, but about Hamlet, who exists only thanks to fortunate collusion between one man who wrote a script and other men who act it out, and still others who read it. No one at the theatre finds this fact esoteric. It is only students of printed texts who are apt to worry about Hamlet's age, or speculate about his experiences at the University (i.e., offstage). The student of printed texts is apt to conjure up all manner of potential difficulties which in practice, in the theatre, trouble no one. Literary people in the eighteenth century supposed that the famous "unities" corresponded to inviolable laws, trespasses against which could reduce a play to mishmash; it remained for Dr Johnson to assert what every frequenter of the playhouse found so self-evident he gave no thought to it, that an audience which can imagine itself in Rome will have no difficulty imagining five minutes later that it is in Alexandria, or for that matter that a jealous man in a play may quite plausibly be inflamed by rudimentary tomfoolery with a handkerchief. We can put this more abstractly, and say that *Antony and Cleopatra* and *Othello* present, when acted, self-sufficient worlds containing their own order of reality, which need not "mean."

So. They are waiting. And they will wait for the duration of the second act as well. We have all waited, perhaps not by a tree at evening or on a country road, but waited. The details are immaterial.

They are waiting "for Godot." Each of us has had his Godot, if only someone from whom, for several days, we have expected a letter.

The substance of the play, in short, is as common a human experience as you can find. This seems hardly worth saying, except that it is so seldom said. To read critics, or to listen to discussion, we might well suppose that the substance of the play was some elusive idea or other, and not a very well expressed idea since there is so much disagreement about what it is.

The substance of the play is waiting, amid uncertainty. If there has never been a play about waiting before, that is because no dramatist before Beckett ever thought of attempting such a thing. It seems contrary to the grain of the theatre, where the normal unit is the event, and where intervals between events are cleverly filled so as to persuade us that the cables are weaving and tightening that shall produce the next event. Throughout much of the *Agamemnon* the audience is waiting, waiting for Agamemnon to be killed. The Chorus too is waiting till a doom shall fall, and Cassandra also is waiting for this to happen, and meanwhile is filling the air with predictions no one will listen to (and she knows that they will not listen; she is under a curse of that order). And Clytemnestra is waiting until it shall be time to kill him. But this is different. Aeschylus's play as it draws toward its climax tugs its climax into the domain of the actual. To wait for the inevitable is a waiting of a different quality, so much so that were Agamemnon not killed the play would seem a fraud. But it is no fraud that Godot does not come.

To wait; and to make the audience share the waiting; and to explicate the quality of the waiting: this is not to be done with "plot," which converges on an event the nonproduction of which will defraud us, nor yet is it to be done by simply filling up stage time: by reading the telephone book aloud for instance. Beckett fills the time with beautifully symmetrical structures.

> In the meantime let us try and converse calmly, since we
>   are incapable of keeping silent.
> You're right, we're inexhaustible.
> It's so we won't think.
> We have that excuse.
> It's so we won't hear.
> We have our reasons.
> All the dead voices.
> They make a noise like wings.
> Like leaves.
> Like sand.
> Like leaves.
>   *Silence.*
> They all speak at once.
> Each to itself.
>   *Silence.*
> Rather they whisper.
> They rustle.
> They murmur.
> They rustle.
>   *Silence.*
> What do they say?
> They talk about their lives.
> To have lived is not enough for them.
> They have to talk about it.
> To be dead is not enough for them.
> It is not sufficient.
>   *Silence.*
> They make a noise like feathers.
> Like leaves.

Like ashes.
Like leaves.
> *Long silence.*

Say something!
I'm trying.
> *Long silence.*

(*in anguish*). Say anything at all!
What do we do now?
Wait for Godot.
Ah!
> *Silence.*

This is awful!

In a beautiful economy of phrasing, like cello music, the voices ask and answer, evoking those strange dead voices that speak, it may be, only in the waiting mind, and the spaced and measured silences are as much a part of the dialogue as the words. And the special qualities of the speakers are never ignored. Estragon insists that these voices rustle, and like leaves; Vladimir, less enslaved by idiom, will have it that they murmur, and like wings, or sand, or feathers, or ashes; but Estragon's simple trope is, thanks to his sheer stubbornness, in each case the last word. And the utterances are gradually reduced from sixteen words to two, and the ritual exchange about waiting for Godot has its ritual termination like an amen, the shortest utterance in the play, the monosyllable "Ah!" It is a splendid duet, to make the hearts of worthy actors sing, and contrary to theatrical custom neither part dominates.

As the speeches are symmetrically assigned, so the two acts are symmetrically constructed, a Pozzo-Lucky incident in each preceding each time the appearance of the boy whose report is that Godot will not come today, "but surely tomorrow." The molecule of the play, its unit of effect, is symmetry, a symmetrical structure: the stage divided into two halves by the tree, the human race (so far as it is presented) divided into two, Didi and Gogo, then into four, Didi-Gogo and Pozzo-Lucky, then, with the boy's arrival, into two again, our sort, Godot's sort. And symmetries encompass opposites as well: Lucky's long speech in act 1, Lucky's utter silence in act 2. And symmetries govern the units of dialogue: at one extreme, the intricate fugue-like structure about the dead sounds and at the other extreme an exchange as short as this:

> We could do our exercises.
> Our movements.
> Our relaxations.
> Our elongations.
> Our relaxations.
> To warm us up.
> To calm us down.
> Off we go.

Or even as short as this:

> How time flies when one has fun!

—three words and three words, pivoted on a "when," and "flies" alliterated with the incongruous "fun."

For nothing satisfies the mind like balance; nothing has so convincing a look of being substantial. The mind recoils from the random. That "honesty is the best policy" seems a self-evident truth chiefly because the words are of metrical equivalence: honesty, policy. Proverbs work like that; sentences, even, work like that, and it is only by a difficult effort of attention, or else by the custom of the Civil Service, that a sentence with no balance can be constructed. Venture to utter a subject, and you will find your mind making ready a predicate that shall balance it. That is why we so seldom ask if lines of poetry make sense: the satisfactions of symmetry intervene. "To be or not to be, that is the question," or: "Tomorrow and tomorrow and tomorrow . . ." or: "The cloud capp'd towers, the gorgeous palaces . . ."—such things derive much authority from equilibrium, and: "In Xanadu did Kubla Khan . . ." exudes magic from its inversion of vowel sequence, -an, -u, -u, -an, despite our uncertainty about three of its five words. Beckett spent much time in his youth with the great virtuoso of such effects, James Joyce, whose last work, a sceptic's model of the universe, may be described as a system of intricate verbal recurrences to none of which a denotative meaning can with any confidence be assigned. And Laurel and Hardy would have been an utterly unconvincing couple were it not for the virtual identity of their hats, two shiny black bowlers.

It is rather from the second act of *Waiting for Godot* than from the first that its finest verbal symmetries can be culled, for the play converges on symmetry:

Say, I am happy.
I am happy.
So am I.
So am I.
We are happy.
We are happy. (*Silence.*) What do we do, now that we are
     happy?
Wait for Godot. (*Estragon groans. Silence.*)

The play also converges on certain very stark statements, the eloquence of which has sometimes left the impression that they are what
the play "means." Thus Pozzo's "They give birth astride of a grave,
the light gleams an instant, then it's night once more," has mani-
fested an unlucky quotability. It is wrung out of Pozzo, in the play,
by Didi's pestiferous questioning. The last straw, elicited by the
discovery that Lucky, who spoke so eloquently in act 1, is "dumb"
in act 2, has been the question, "Dumb! Since when?" Whereupon
Pozzo (*"suddenly furious"*) bursts out:

> Have you not done tormenting me with your accursed
> time! It's abominable! When! When! One day, is that not
> enough for you, one day he went dumb, one day I went
> blind, one day we'll go deaf, one day we were born, one
> day we shall die, the same day, the same second, is that not
> enough for you? (*Calmer.*) They give birth astride of a
> grave, the light gleams an instant, then it's night once
> more. (*He jerks the rope.*) On!

This is to say, as so many things are to say, that we cannot be sure
the play's two days are successive; to say that there are many days
like these, that all waiting is endless, and all journeying. The striking
metaphor is like Pozzo, that connoisseur of rhetoric. It sticks in
Didi's mind, and a few minutes later, alone with the sleeping Gogo,
he is reflecting that he too may be sleeping, so dream-like is the
tedium.

> Tomorrow, when I wake, or think I do, what shall I say of
> to-day? That with Estragon my friend, at this place, until
> the fallof night, I waited for Godot? That Pozzo passed,
> with his carrier, and that he spoke to us? Probably. But in
> all that what truth will there be?

Then he repeats the figure Pozzo used:

> Astride of a grave and a difficult birth. Down in the hole, lingeringly, the grave-digger puts on the forceps. We have time to grow old. The air is full of our cries. (*He listens.*) But habit is a great deadener. (*He looks again at Estragon.*) At me too someone is looking, of me too someone is saying, He is sleeping, he knows nothing, let him sleep on. (*Pause.*) I can't go on! (*Pause.*) What have I said?

This is rather an aesthetic than a didactic climax, as the force and beauty of the language should indicate, and the strange figure of serial watchers. Didi is watching Gogo, we in the auditorium are watching Didi (though not saying that he is sleeping), someone invisible watches us all in turn: this evokes less a Deity than an infinite series. Like music, Beckett's language is shaped into phrases, orchestrated, cunningly repeated. The statements it makes have torque within the work's context and only there, while the form, the symmetry, ministers to the form of the work, its wholeness, its uniqueness. We find other, quite different things said in quite different plays and novels of Beckett's, never wildly optimistic things it is true, but never ambitious of reaching outside the structure in which they are contained. It is that structure, shaped, sometimes self-cancelling if it pleases him, that he has laboured to perfect, draft after draft. And like all of us he has habitual attitudes. After years of familiarity with his work, I find no sign that it has ambitions to enunciate a philosophy of life. Nor had Stan Laurel.

The Waiting Since

Richard Gilman

By now there is a large body of criticism of Beckett's theater, some of it of a very high order: Jacques Guicharnaud's, Hugh Kenner's, Ruby Cohn's, among writings in English. But like that of the fiction, this criticism often suffers from a scanting of the works' aesthetic reality, their mysterious functioning as drama, in favor of their being seen as closed philosophical utterances, histrionic forms of the vision Beckett had previously shaped into intense, arid tales, structures of intellectual despair placed on stage. Or else, if they are accepted as proper dramas, they are made local, particularized into anecdotes or fables of circumscribed and idiosyncratic conditions.

Thus an observer as acute and wrongheaded as Norman Mailer could detect the motif of impotence in *Waiting for Godot* but interpret it as sexual, delivering the play over to his own anxious concerns and so brutally shrinking its dimensions. In the same way an astute critic like the Yugoslavian scholar Darko Suvin can call Beckett's entire theater "relevant" only in "random and closed situations of human existence: in war, camps, prisons, sickness, old age, grim helplessness." Yet if these plays are not "relevant" to everything, coherent with human situations everywhere, then they are merely peripheral games of the imagination, grim and transient jests. But they are nothing of the kind.

When *En attendant Godot* opened in Paris in the spring of 1953, it was received with widespread incomprehension and even revul-

From *The Making of Modern Drama.* © 1972, 1973, 1974 by Richard Gilman. Farrar, Straus & Giroux, 1974.

sion on the part of the general public and the conventional press, and with great praise, amounting in places to a kind of ecstatic gratefulness, by a number of influential persons who were able to assure it a modest commercial success. Jean Anouilh, who thought the opening the most important in Paris since that of Pirandello's *Six Characters* thirty years before, described the play in one of the first reviews to appear as "the music-hall sketch of Pascal's *Pensées* as played by the Fratellini clowns," a characterization that has never been improved upon. And the playwright Armand Salacrou spoke of it in another early review as the fulfillment of a generation's hopes and expectancies: "We were waiting for this play of our time, with its new tone, its simple and modest language, and its closed, circular plot from which no exit is possible."

The play was presented in America several years later, in Beckett's own English translation. He had started writing in French in 1945 with a novel, *Mercier et Camier* (which has just been published), after naturally having written his first poems, fiction, and the essay *Proust* in his native language. Asked on several occasions why he had turned to French, in which he had in fact become wholly fluent during the seventeen years since he had come to Paris following his graduation from Dublin's Trinity College in 1927, he replied once that "I just felt like it. It was a different experience from writing in English," and another time, much more pointedly, that it was because "you couldn't help writing poetry in English." French, the more severe, emotionally limited language, suited his new intentions more closely.

Waiting for Godot was a commercial failure in the United States in 1956. Its critical reception was very much like that in France: bewilderment and distaste among the middle-brow reviewers, intense enthusiasm in avant-garde circles. Marya Mannes wrote a representative notice: "I doubt whether I have seen a worse play. I mention it only as typical of the self-delusion of which certain intellectuals are capable, embracing obscurity, pretense, ugliness and negation as protective coloring for their own confusions." Norman Mailer wrote two reviews for the newly founded *Village Voice*. The first was a scornful attack, the second, a week later, a grudging admission that the play had something after all. He added, however, that he still believed that "most of the present admirers of *Godot* are . . . snobs, intellectual snobs of undue ambition and impotent imagination, the worst sort of literary type, invariably more interested in being part of some intellectual elite than in the creative act itself."

This peculiar emphasis on what was considered to be the effeteness and self-deception of both Beckett and his admirers was characteristic at the time, and was only gradually moved to the fringes of cultural history as a die-hard position of know-nothingism when the years passed and Beckett's genius and his enormous influence on younger writers became evident to nearly everyone. The phenomenon of course resembles the various stages of reaction to Joyce and more broadly to modern art and literature in all their successive movements. In this case an idea of dramatic procedure was being violated; the theater, which was supposed to be an emotional matter, to present images of action, was being employed for inaction, and its tradition of completions and endings was being flouted by an almost intolerable irresolution. These things more than the play's ostensible "content," its melancholy view of human power and possibility, were what so disturbed conventional minds (or minds which like Mailer's had large areas of conventionality).

If *Waiting for Godot* is now widely accepted as the greatest dramatic achievement of the last generation, some would say the greatest imaginative work of any kind during the period, it is obviously because its once radically new form has with time been assimilated into educated consciousness, becoming at last a kind of norm itself. Diderot once wrote that "if one kind of art exists, it is difficult to have another kind," and Alain Robbe-Grillet has described the difficulty more precisely: "A new form always seems to be more or less an absence of any form at all, since it is unconsciously judged by reference to consecrated forms."

The new forms or dramatic methods that Beckett and others introduced in the early fifties found their own consecration in the collective designation Theater of the Absurd; along with Eugène Ionesco, whose work his in fact scarcely resembles, Beckett continues to be identified as one of that artificially created "movement's" chief practitioners. Dissimilar as their plays are, Beckett and Ionesco did however share a common ground in the abandonment of sequential action (their ancestors, though not their conscious influences, being Büchner and the early Brecht), their exclusion of almost everything that could be thought of as plot, and their creation of a general atmosphere of illogic, of not "adding up." If anything, Ionesco's first plays satisfied more strictly than did Beckett's the dictionary definition of absurdity as being "that which is contrary to reason"; Beckett's dramas have always been closer to Camus's meaning in his description of the absurd as "that divorce between the mind that desires and the world that disappoints."

This separation between desire and reality is in the largest sense what *Waiting for Godot* is about; it is a play of absence, a drama whose binding element is what *does not take place.* The fierce paradox of this provoked the search for the identity of the Godot of the title, as a way of uncovering the play's meaning, that became a minor critical industry in France and elsewhere. Richard Coe and others have found the source of the name in a well-known French racing cyclist, Godeau; Eric Bentley has pointed out the existence of an obscure play of Balzac's in which someone named Godeaux is expected throughout the evening but never arrives; and Roger Blin has said that Beckett told him the name comes from the French slang word for boot— *godillot*—and was chosen simply because of the importance in the play of boots and shoes as physical properties.

It has become clear that whatever the origin of the name, Godot is not to be sought outside the boundaries of the play itself, just as he is not to be encountered within them. What the two tramps do encounter is his possibility; they are held to their places, their stripped, rudimentary existence on "a country road" with its single tree, at evening, by the possibility that he will come to them or summon them to him, and their task, we might call it their *raison d'être,* is just to wait. The play was originally called simply *Waiting,* and there is a significant clue in the final French title: *"en" attendant,* "while" waiting. The drama is about what Vladimir and Estragon do while waiting for Godot, who does not come, whose very nature is that he doesn't come. He is a sought-for transcendency, that which is desired beyond our physical lives, so that these may have meaning.

But the meaning, the validation the tramps seek for their lives is never forthcoming; there is no transcendent being or realm from which human justification proceeds, or rather—and this is the crucial difference between *Waiting for Godot* and so many modern works of despair—we cannot be sure whether there is or not. In the space this doubt creates, Didi and Gogo exist, neither "saved" nor "damned," unable to leave, which is to say, unable not to exist, held there by an unbearable tension which it is their task—or rather the play's task; the play as formal human invention—to make bearable. Godot is not a figure for God or for immortality or, conversely, for the absence of these; he or it is a term within an imagined structure of life as we would feel or experience it if we were reduced, as Didi and Gogo are, to sheer, naked, noncontingent being, without theories, rationalizations, or abstract consolations of any kind.

For as Jacques Guicharnaud has said, the figure of the tramp represents "man as such, as detached from society," and so from the mental and behavioral constructions by which social organization hides from us our real condition. Society is by nature optimistic, progressive (in the sense that it moves forward, develops new forms, believes that it improves), and self-sufficient. Man beyond (or beneath) society is pitched past such categories as optimism and pessimism, is existentially static (except that he moves physically toward death), and is radically insufficient. *Waiting for Godot* is a drama of man in such a state. It thus resembles in its themes and attitudes a number of plays of the modern past: *Peer Gynt,* with its motif of the destruction of the self through a belief in its sufficiency; *The Three Sisters,* with its static extension of lives that do not find culminations; *Baal,* with its protagonist placed beyond society's laws and claims.

But since the state with which all these plays from one perspective or another deal is itself an abstraction from the *real world,* since man only exists physically in society or by reference to it—as in the case of a hermit or a shipwrecked person—the dramatic imagination has to create, as a gesture toward reality and to fulfill the requirements of drama itself, some kind of social ground. That is to say, there has to be exchange, community of some sort, dialogue; in a paradox that is at the heart of the theater's art, the state of noncontingent existence, of pure being, together with the feeling of what it is like to be alive whatever the circumstances, is rendered only through contingencies and circumstances. Without these a play would be a philosophical disquisition, just as without the presence of at least two characters it would be a solipsistic exercise. We shall see how in all Beckett's plays the necessity of there being more than one character is met, even if, as in *Krapp's Last Tape,* the "other" is simply the one's recorded past self.

Vladimir and Estragon are thus linked together by something much more mysterious and elemental than what we think of as friendship. The connection is of an imaginative and metaphysical order; they are under the obligation *to be two,* a pair, a social unit outside society. "Don't touch me! Don't question me! Don't speak to me! Stay with me!" Estragon abjures Vladimir at one point. And when one or the other, but especially Estragon, the somewhat more spontaneous and childlike of the two, expresses a desire to leave his companion, he is unable to, just as neither can break the invisible bond that ties them to the possibility of Godot's coming.

For to leave each other or to quit the place where they have been told to wait (by whom or what? by the intention of the playwright, communicated to them as his creations) would be a contradiction of the terms of their existence. This is a difficult notion for us, who have been nurtured on the value of free will, which is at its most sovereign in literature and drama. There characters must be seen to act freely, to bring about their own fates however disastrous, or else be thought of as pawns in a mechanical, unlifelike game. That Didi and Gogo are as "lifelike" in their way as the characters of classical drama and far more so than those of a debased classicism, such as the modern conventional theater had been offering, is one basis of the play's stature, its new beauty.

Their lifelikeness on the stage derives from their very unfreedom, or rather from their attitude toward it. To begin with, they do not question it, since that would mean they could be something other than what they are—the men who must wait. And in the face of this unfathomable compulsion to remain where they are, they devise—it is the exact word—a provisional, tactical liberty, one of speech and small gestures. They are like prisoners free to amuse one another or to take advantage of the penitentiary's game room, the crucial difference being that for them the prison walls are as wide as the earth. No *idea* of existence itself being free afflicts or consoles them; and their wit and raillery, their wry or bitter utterance within this larger unfreedom, give them their dignity, for if they do not rebel, neither do they quietly submit.

Held there then, without a say in the matter, they must contrive to exist, not hopelessly, but in a strange sort of indeterminacy in which hope is not an emotion or state of mind but an absence of proof that one ought to despair. And they must fill out this existence, which stretches from a vague historical beginning—they speak of having been together perhaps fifty years, of having once been "respectable," and of having been "in the Macon country"—to an unknown end, through their own resources, unaided and unjustified by anything outside themselves.

In this regard they are almost wholly theatrical, for in its essence theater is that which shows us life being fabricated, so to speak, from scratch; when an actor steps onto a stage, he appears to have emerged as by spontaneous generation and he must live in this artificial environment by the inventions—the created words and gestures—of the playwright. What modern realism had done (and continues to do), however, was to disguise behind a multiplicity of detail, a surface of likeness to our ordinary lives, this radical nakedness and *ab ovo* quality of both theater and the life it is designed to illumine. One central strand of *Waiting for Godot*'s originality is its having recovered a lost principle of theater at the same time as it displays us to ourselves in our root condition.

It is the tramps' *presence* on the stage which, like ours on the earth, is at bottom unaccountable; as Robbe-Grillet has written, "They must explain themselves," defending their right to be there, although the plea is not offered to any judge or jury but to the void, which it helps to fill. Once again the connection between theater and life is intimate. The tramps are compelled to speak, are indeed, as Estragon says, "incapable of keeping silent," just as we are, since it is only through our words, those most abstract and insubstantial of our possessions, that we overcome—temporarily and with an illusory solace—our actor-like isolation and sense of arbitrary being.

And so a great deal of *Waiting for Godot* is conversation, between Didi and Gogo in large part, between them and the boy (or boys) who brings news of Godot, and between them and Pozzo (whose significance along with that of his servant Lucky will be taken up shortly). The conversation, like that proposed in *Murphy*, means to be "without precedent in fact or literature, each one speaking to the best of his ability the truth to the best of his knowledge." The ability the tramps possess is that of sheer verbal invention; it is as though they ad-lib for their very lives, talking endlessly for fear of the annihilation silence would bring, "keeping the ball rolling" between them in an action which gives them the necessary "illusion that they exist." And the truth they utter is not about anything external to themselves or even about their internal state; *Waiting for Godot* doesn't give information of the world or of the emotions or psyche but of what it is like to "be there," to have to be.

In doing this it offers no meanings in the traditional sense, an absence which is the source of its being designated "absurd." Like Beckett's fiction, the play works tirelessly against just that desire for explicit meaning that has so often forced literature and the theater into a pedagogic function at odds with their aesthetic one. "I do not teach, I am a witness," Ionesco has said, a remark that applies with even more pertinence to Beckett and his tramps. For neither he nor they know why they are waiting or for whom ("If I had known who Godot is, I would have said," Beckett has told us); all they know is that they do not know and that the hole their ignorance makes, Pascal's void felt at one's fingertips, must be filled in by words, the way space is filled by a juggler's balls or an acrobat's parabola.

Such analogies to the world of the circus and the music hall have often been made in regard to Beckett's theater, Hugh Kenner having gone so far as to locate the antecedents of his plays not in previous drama but in "Emmett Kelly's solemn determination to sweep a circle of light into a dustpan." The perception is shrewd but is a bit beyond the mark. For while the plays do indeed rise from the atmosphere and morale of circus rings and vaudeville stages, as well as from those of American silent-film comedy, their historic action is to have used those sources for a regeneration of theatrical art, whose elemental shapes and procedures were always firmly in Beckett's grasp. It was the desperate nonsense, the splendidly adroit accomplishment of insignificant acts (in a literal sense: without meaning or use) of trapeze artists, one-man bands, and people who stand on their index fingers—or the equally grand failure on the part of clowns and stooges to attain the simplest physical results—that Beckett borrowed in order to compose dramas of immediate presence as opposed to narrative unfoldings and of gratuitous being instead of portentous humanistic conviction.

These influences are much more directly physical than verbal in *Waiting for Godot*: the bowlers and baggy pants, the ill-fitting shoes and difficulties with laces, the carrots and turnips—fundamental, inane foods eaten like haute cuisine—the vaudeville routine of exchanging hats, the general impression of a succession of "turns" being done, unsequential, self-contained epiphanies of corporeal wisdom and folly. But the speech also emerges shaped and ordered like a program on an announcement board: now we say this, now we say that, we fill up the time. In actuality the circus is a place of pure physicality, as is of course the silent screen, and what Beckett has done, the essence of his innovating or renovating method, is to have thrown language, the chief bearer of our weighty significances, into a physical world of farcical gesture and knockabout comedy whose effect is to undermine all intellectual pretensions. One cannot speak "meaningfully" with a turnip in one's mouth and wearing shoes two sizes too big or too small.

In the same way that the "meaning" of the circus and of physical comedy is in their relation to the sober significances we attach to everything else in life, that of *Waiting for Godot* is in its relation to the values of logic, purposefulness, psychic or moral revelation, etc., we have been trained to expect from drama. Like the clown and the tap dancer, Didi and Gogo instruct us, by their improvisatory presence, in unseriousness, in a revivifying frivolity whose desperate edge is the result of a recognition that it is covering over an abyss. Their talk is not so much anti-intellectual as counterintellectual; in the course of the play they mock or demolish all our myths of meaning, using language against itself so as to prevent it from disguising their radical vulnerability. After an absurdly grave exchange about radishes, Didi says, "This is becoming really insignificant," to which Gogo replies, "Not enough."

This process of what we might call a decantation of meaning is continuous in the play, which takes up themes of many kinds—religious, philosophical, psychological—without allowing any of them to become the drama's motif, and with a fierce comic opposition to their pretensions. "We have kept our appointment and that's an end to that," Didi orates at one point. "We are not saints, but we have kept our appointment. How many people can boast as much?" Gogo's wonderfully deflating reply is "Billions." In another exchange Didi asserts, "We are happy," words which Gogo mechanically repeats before asking, "What do we do now, now that we are happy?" Didi's answer is a pressure back to the naked ground of their existence, beneath emotions, psychic particularities, or humanist values: "Wait for Godot."

Beyond this, language and gesture are in a wholly ambiguous causal relationship. In another break with dramatic tradition, speech does not predict gesture or gesture speech. Instead of instigating physical actions or articulating their relevances, language now operates to ignore, question, or annul them. The most striking examples of this are the last lines of both acts—"Yes, let's go"—which are followed in the text by the words "They do not move" and on the stage by the tramps remaining immobile. There is no explanation of the failure to stir, only the presence of the gap. In this way the orderly universe of utterance followed by logically related movement, of volition succeeded by steps taken, which we inhabit as our very air, is disrupted, pulled asunder. And in the spaces this leaves we feel comically and harrowingly deprived of support, for here language, instead of controlling or shaping the world, has established its own wayward dominion.

Pozzo and Lucky. These two are emissaries from the realm of time and from the life of society, with its institutionalized relationships, its comforts and delusions, above all its thirst for hierarchies. Didi and Gogo live in an atmosphere in which time barely moves forward and in which all values are flattened out under the arc of Godot's possibility, the value whose absence empties all judgments. Here one thing is as important or as unimportant as any other—a carrot or a memory, a shoe or love—and here nothing has power over anything else. In Pozzo and Lucky, on the contrary, are embodied the very principles of human power and exploitation, delusory, ultimately disastrous, but maintained by them as the foundation of their lives.

They are thus a contrast to the tramps' perpetually self-invented, powerless beings, which hunger for a net under the void in whose air they dance, like cartoon characters arrested in mid-fall from a cliff. For Pozzo and Lucky are creatures of the society from which Didi and Gogo have been extricated in order that they may wait, without histories or plans, for validation. Agents of "reality," these intruders have been shaped by its exigencies and values, which divert us from our condition of helplessness, and by time, which blinds us to our fateful, deep lack of change. Unexpected signs of Beckett's genius, their presence in the play helps, along with the brogans and radishes, to preserve it from an overbuoyancy, a lightness arising from its deprivation of the ordinary materials and weights of "realistic" drama. They are reminders of the actuality the imagination has to leave behind.

In the way Godot's identity has been sought for and worried over, those of Pozzo and Lucky have been traced to numerous objective sources. Bertolt Brecht is said to have been planning at his death a socialist version of the play in which Pozzo would incarnate capitalist exploitation and Lucky proletarian subjection. More broadly, Lucky's relationship to Pozzo has been taken to be that of intellect enslaved by materialism, and the former's presence with a rope around his neck (the mind at the end of its tether) and his famous speech—a broken, mad onrush of scraps of theology, philosophy, and scientific information—do suggest some such structure. But there is a danger in this kind of interpretative pursuit. *Waiting for Godot* is no allegory but a marvelously concrete work to which we are asked to lend our senses, our unrationalized affective capacities as spectators; the social or political relevance may or may not follow.

The difficulty is of course that we are used to experiencing in drama emotions we have felt in life, enhanced and given formal structure on the stage, and that these emotions are always attached to narrative situations, however brief or self-contained. We live by telling ourselves tales out of the materials of our experience or reveries: stories of love, hatred, moral or physical triumph or disaster, anecdotes of happiness or regret, all with progressive movements and outcomes, endings. But there is no recognizable story in *Waiting for Godot* and hence no development, no suspensefulness (except that of whether or not Godot will come; but to respond to the play at all is to understand at once that he will not), and no denouement, the very principles of dramatic interest, as we have been taught.

Moreover, the emotions that are thus offered in suspension, as it were, are continually balked, stifled, canceled out. Whenever a character appears to be feeling some definite emotion or to have entered some decisive area of commitment, it is all undone, by an opposing remark, a corrosive scornfulness, a physical jape. This process of undoing is also one of the chief functions of Beckett's famous pauses and silences, intervals of emptiness which resemble those in Chekhov and which in both playwrights serve as agencies of negation or ironic undermining. In one sequence Gogo asks "if we're tied." "To Godot?" Didi replies. "Tied to Godot. What an idea! No question of it. (*Pause.*) For the moment." Into the pause rushes our own awareness that there is every question of it, and Didi's subsequent "For the moment" simply adds a further irony to the exchange.

The result of all this is that we find it difficult to "identify" with the tramps, and this will be true as long as we wish them to be traditional protagonists carrying forward an active narrative full of recognizable events to a point of resolution and summing up. We have to see them as figures provisionally outside time and cumulative circumstances, placed on stage in order to show us what being on earth, beneath social fate and personal distinctiveness, is like. As Büchner made Woyzeck into an embodiment of pure oppressed creatureliness, the victim as hero, Strindberg split his characters into faculties and impulses, and Chekhov kept his three sisters immobile so that their truthfulness as survivors might be seen—all blows at dramatic rules and rubrics—so Beckett, in the most far-reaching revolution of all, deprives his characters of a story and an ending in order to demonstrate how we wait for these things, how the waiting is our bitter, comic task.

Yet the demonstration is no abstract exercise but a form of invented life, and this life at the extremity moves us deeply in ways we could not have foreseen. We have not had these emotions, for we have not knowingly lived this existence; but we recognize it now. There are moments in the play of great poignancy—it is the wrong word, but this is Beckett, in which no word is ever quite "right"— when we fully intuit the mysterious unexampled humanity of the entire work and are moved to tears through our laughter. Perhaps the deepest of these occasions are when the Boy appears at the end of each act with word that Godot will not come "today." "What am I to tell Mr. Godot, Sir?" he asks them once. Didi's reply contains the essence of the longing, the uncertainty, and the painfulness of this clown show, this juggling act in stricken space: "Tell him . . . (*He hesitates.*) . . . tell him you saw us."

The Language of Myth

Bert O. States

> I am interested in the shape of ideas even if I do not believe in them. There
> is a wonderful sentence in Augustine. I wish I could remember the Latin. It
> is even finer in Latin than in English. "Do not despair; one of the thieves
> was saved. Do not presume; one of the thieves was damned." That sentence
> has a wonderful shape. It is the shape that matters.
>
> SAMUEL BECKETT

My epigraph is more than a poetic or philosophical perspective on
my subject: it is the subject itself. My aim here will be to examine the
respects in which the Augustine paradox imitates the "shape" of
Waiting for Godot—is, in fact, a perfect working model of the play's
structural dialectic.

I will be concerned in later chapters with the theological idea
that is lodged in the paradox, but perhaps, for the record, it would
be well to show its general relevance to the play. *Godot,* one might
say, is about the two thieves, or rather about the idea posed by the
parable of the two thieves. For we are dealing here not only with
characters and events—say Vladimir and Estragon, who, as far as we
know, have no such destiny as crucifixion (and all that follows)—but
with the odds or "percentages" of salvation versus damnation for the
race. In short, the two thieves who die with Christ are nothing more,
or less, than momentary symbols of the theme that is the subject, in
one way or another, of all the Scriptures. It is almost too awesome
a theme to be dealt with outside the devotional sanctity of allegory,
and allegory, as Beckett says in *Proust,* always fails in the hands of a
poet. Given the modern mood, moreover, it would even seem that

Beckett the poet undertook it at a certain risk which lingers, one critical syllable beyond allegory, in the very title of the play. It is a big dangerous theme, this theme of themes. As Coleridge stunningly sums it up, "A Fall of some sort or other—the creation, as it were, of the non-absolute—is the fundamental postulate of the moral history of man. Without this hypothesis, man is unintelligible; with it, every phenomenon is explicable. The mystery itself is too profound for human insight." Or, as Vladimir might say, "It's too much for one man." And that is the danger: it is almost too profound for "the boards." One cannot come at it with too secure a belief or it degenerates into doctrine, and, if justice is to be done to its profundity, one cannot come at it with too devastating an irony. What made Beckett the ideal modern to write a play about "The Fall"—as opposed, say, to Claudel, on one hand, or Ionesco, on the other—is that his peculiar skepticism of all firm positions rescued him (in this play at least) from both the artistic sin of Faith and the shallowness of an easy despair. Which is to say that he chose Augustine's paradox of the two thieves and not the moralistic version in Luke in which salvation and damnation are distributed on the basis of conduct (one thief reviled Christ and was, apparently, damned; one confessed and was, apparently, saved). Hence that fascinating sentence—*it is the shape that matters*—standing provocatively beneath the mystery of the cross.

Put simply, this essay is an examination of the ways in which shape matters in *Godot*. This comes down, mainly, to a problem of language and its function as an ordering principle of the play's master myth. In other words, I am not concerned with the *poetry* in the language or with an interpretation of the play but with the structure of its intelligibility. In some ways, the essay is an extension of a problem in poetics I dealt with recently in a study of *Hamlet:* that is, the way in which a fiction teaches us to fill in details that are not there at all and do so in the style of those that are. What I was chiefly interested in was the thickness of *Hamlet*'s world as communicated by the unusual diversity and density of its imagery, or what I called word pictures. This thickness, I suggested, has a significant effect on our options for interpreting the play; for it is primarily through imagery, or linguistically established "scenery," that we derive our sense of the qualitative range of a play's world, its limits and possibilities, the kinds of things that can take place in its spatial and temporal environment.

More recently, I used *Hamlet* as the central text of a seminar as a means of grounding certain principles of Shakespeare's art and dramatic art in general. It occurred to me that one way of illuminating *Hamlet*'s style (in the more inclusive sense of the word) would be to put it flat against the text of a dramatist who was working at the other stylistic extreme while treating similar thematic issues. In short, through the neutralizing effects of a double perspective we might minimize the risks of losing the unique sense of a writer in the familiar and seductive jungle of his own "closed" world. With respect to style alone, the perfect antithesis of *Hamlet* is *Waiting for Godot,* the modern play, above all others, which seems to involve us in these same risks of overfamiliarity to an especially high degree— perhaps for the same reason that they run so high in *Hamlet:* that is, a certain archetypal richness which makes it all but impossible to read the play as anything but an icon of a permanent racial enigma.

What impresses one about *Godot* (in contrast to *Hamlet*) is the linguistic spareness of its world. Whereas in *Hamlet* a single image is apt to get lost in a crowded universe of images and to become significant, or thematic, through frequent variation and repetition, in *Godot* the image achieves an instant significance by virtue of occurring—and often only once—in an "empty" space, or one in which it obtrudes suddenly from a language texture composed of seemingly random or diversionary conversation. It is this quality of randomness that creates the paradoxical impression of an unplanned design. In fact, if we were to condense *Godot* to a graphic illustration of itself, it might resemble a highly "successful" Rorschach blot. I am not thinking of its possible diagnostic values or of a particular shape it might take (say, three vaguely crosslike forms); rather, I have in mind the simple wonder of the blot's appeal: like Found Art, it is unintentionally provocative; not a created object but a creative one, or better still, no object at all but a concatenation of possibilities, limited by nothing but the mind's capacity to endow shape with meaning. In other words, in the blot principle we confront the very algebra of imagination; in a flash of form we bypass the whole realm of factual equivalence and enter a world where structural affinity is the only law governing identity. This also happens to be the world of dreams and myth, and my more specific aim here is to examine the extraordinary mythic "pull" of this play from the standpoint of its formal allurements which, I would argue, are roughly analogous to the hide-and-seek artistry of the Rorschach blot.

To qualify the analogy a bit further, I am hardly implying that

Beckett, or any playwright, could be unintentionally provocative with any success. What I mean is that the shapes and subshapes in *Godot* behave *as if* they were. No sooner do we begin the play than we are in the presence of a massive duplicity which is at once the source of its peculiar openness and its resistance to interpretation. Everything has a way of meaning something and at the same time blurring any clear sign of representational intention. This is not simply the normal ambiguity of symbol systems but a kind of flatness or indifference in the text which provokes an extraordinary creative indulgence in the reader (a critical syndrome we might liken to Rapture of the Deep). The perfect novelistic parallel might be Kafka. Some years ago there was a book on Kafka which studiously traced Kafka's oedipal obsessions through his imagery and, getting enraptured in the possibilities, ended by converting everything in sight to sexual membership (with the result that at one point in *The Castle* a wooden plank was copulating with an open window). This is the sort of excess Kafka inspires and it is, if anything, even more rampant in the Beckett criticism, especially that of *Godot*. And it has to do, obviously, with the peculiar stirrings that occur when "realism" and "symbolism" meet in powerfully mythic imaginations; that is, when an ontological parable is pulsating beneath a deceptive crust of actuality. Beckett's play, like Kafka's novels, would be unbearably boring were it not for the fact that its visible actuality, its text, is only a sham surface beneath which universal ideas are constantly generating, only to squirt away like tomato seeds under the finger of definition. We can say of *Godot* exactly what Roland Barthes says of Kafka's narrative: "[It] authorizes a thousand equally plausible keys—which is to say, it validates none."

One of the most pervasive sources of this "mythic" effect is the play's way of speaking to us (or to no one) through its characters who, with one key exception I will discuss in the final chapter, are continually missing the point of their own conversation: they talk on the subject but have no idea what the subject is; they think they are waiting for a man named Godot or for night, literally, to fall. Even when a loaded, or intentional, image passes their lips it does so oxymoronically, with a profound triviality. For example:

> ESTRAGON: What about hanging ourselves?
> POZZO: . . . What is your name?
> ESTRAGON: Adam.

POZZO: . . . Of the same species as Pozzo! Made in
God's image!

Or, to take a more substantial passage which will serve as a locus of overall style:

VLADIMIR: I tell you his name is Pozzo.
ESTRAGON: We'll soon see. (*He reflects.*) Abel! Abel!
POZZO: Help!
ESTRAGON: Got it in one!
VLADIMIR: I begin to weary of this motif.
ESTRAGON: Perhaps the other is called Cain. Cain! Cain!
POZZO: Help!
ESTRAGON: He's all humanity. (*Silence.*) Look at the little
cloud.
VLADIMIR: (*raising his eyes*) Where?
ESTRAGON: There. In the zenith.
VLADIMIR: Well? (*Pause.*) What is there so wonderful
about it?
Silence.
ESTRAGON: Let's pass on now to something else, do you
mind?

Here the play is suddenly astir with mythical depth. As through one of those perspective windows in a Renaissance painting, an ancient scene arises. But it is swallowed, just as suddenly, in what the play advertises as its subject: the boredom of waiting. If we examine this boredom from the standpoint of the play's deeper strategy, however, we see that it is a disguise beneath which we detect the author making a halfhearted escape, as if having gone too far toward being explicit ("accidentally on purpose"), he overreacts and trivializes his image, literally, in this case, clouding it over. All in all, it is much the same tactic Iago uses on Othello: plant the truth by casually naming it, then urgently taking it back.

The question is, what truth, exactly, has been planted? Obviously, in this play, Abel and Cain are images of a very high priority. The trouble is, they come and go so fast that they can only be treated in slow motion, and it is precisely the speed of their passing that produces the hide-and-seek effect. As a contrast, think of the leisurely "classical" scene in which Hamlet picks up the skull in the graveyard and imagines it, among other things, to be "Cain's jawbone, that did the first murder." The keynote of this style, here as everywhere in Shakespeare, is in the forthrightness and precision of focus. The idea is marching openly on the surface of the text and there is no doubt about what is meant: what more apt example of "all humanity" en route to the grave than that of the first murderer mortified? There is no contrivance, no obliquity; or rather, the contrivance is laid bare as a conflation of author and character. Though Shakespeare cannot be identified editorially with Hamlet, there is a sense in which his own intentions come snugly to rest in Hamlet's eloquence. Quite naturally, the play has given birth to this skull through the urgency of its own pregnancy with death; and quite naturally Hamlet elaborates its meanings. Our thinking, you might say, is done for us and we are free to admire the thought.

What is altogether absent in the Cain scene from *Godot* is just this forthright point of intellection; there is no *processing* consciousness which gives to the text a final authority. Cain and Abel appear only latently, the code words of a certain rich history involving (if we pause to explicate) all sorts of thematic "shapes" relevant to the play: ownership of land, inhumanity, divine preferment and punishment, exile, wandering over the land, God's vengeful withdrawal from men's sight, etc. In short, there is a wave of unspecified meaning here and it produces, on its abrupt retreat, an undertow of the sort that one feels most powerfully in the presence of myth.

Actually, the mythic quality of this image has less to do with the story of Abel and Cain than with something much less tangible. If we think about the image for a moment, we see that it does not settle at all neatly onto Pozzo or the Pozzo/Lucky situation (as, for example, Cain becomes momentarily synonymous with the skull in Hamlet's hand). The act of brother-murder for which Cain and Abel are famous contains far too much overkill to serve as a metaphor for Pozzo's victimization of Lucky, which we are invited to associate with it. There is also the good possibility that the image does not refer to Pozzo and Lucky at all, or not only to them, but to Vladimir and Estragon who are, in this scene, committing something of an outrage on their fellowmen. In fact, earlier in this act there is another oblique reference to Cain and Abel which does exactly this and we should probably add it here since it illustrates this same hide-and-seek tactic in reverse:

ESTRAGON: The best thing would be to kill me, like the
    other.
VLADIMIR: What other? (*Pause.*) What other?
ESTRAGON: Like billions of others.
VLADIMIR: (*sententious*) To every man his little cross.

Here we have a clear case of fratricide but the criminal escapes in the crowd. This "other" must certainly be Cain (or Abel) in which case we should probably credit Estragon with having an Adamic fixation, in addition to his Christ complex. More to the point, however, is why he should be so cryptic with Vladimir. In fact, the image (if we can call it that) is virtually dragged into this "simple" argument and carefully framed before being dropped. In other words, the master criminal here seems to be Beckett who steals his myth without actually naming it.

The point about such images is that they do not attach descriptively to characters or situations. Once out of a character's mouth they hover in the air of the play nonreferentially, the property of the play's idea. I don't mean to underrate the aptness of Beckett's images, but they are apt in a peculiar way. To illustrate: there is an old and rather Beckettesque joke about a factory employee who smuggled wheelbarrows past the night watchman by loading them with excelsior and hauling them right through the gate; that is, he deviated the watchman's attention from "the product" to its function, from the valuable to the valueless. Now the particulars of the Cain/Abel myth are far from valueless since, as we have seen, they form a strong constellation of latent meanings; but they do have a kind of excelsior-expendability which is reenforced, in part, by the throwaway tone. It is as if Cain and Abel had been chosen more for the fact of their fame than for the manner in which they earned it. In other words, they mask an even bigger theft and it is that of the entire Old Testament, that whole legendary Ur-world whose figures all possess in common a special family significance by virtue of their direct participation in the divine mystery. They are, in Erich Auerbach's phrase, "fraught with background," and it is this background, in all its priority and permanence, which is made momentarily visible in the figures of Abel and Cain, much as the violent history of the earth is made visible in a single outcropping of rock.

All in all, the vast gulf between the trivial and the profound levels of meaning in the play offers an interpretive summons that is almost identical in principle to the figural interpretation of the Scriptures. That is, a *figura* is a "deceptive form" of something else. "The relation between the two events"—I quote now from Auerbach's essay, *"Figura"*—"is revealed by an accord or similarity. . . . Often vague similarities in the structure of events or in their attendant circumstances suffice to make the *figura* recognizable. (Thus Adam is a *figura* of Christ, the Edenic tree a *figura* of the cross, etc.) All this proceeds from the figural notion that God knows "no difference in time" (to quote Augustine) and therefore everything in the spiritual history of man—from God's point of view anyway—happens "concurrently simultaneously" (to quote Lucky). What I mean in applying this principle to *Godot* is that the play, on its most profound, or theological, level, depicts a further stage of the dilemma of "waiting" that originates with the Expulsion, is passed up through Adam's children in countless stories and parables which, as Auerbach says, are "enacted according to an ideal model which is a prototype situated in the future."

With this biblical world established, virtually from the title forward, as the play's "background" and kept intermittently in the picture by casual (or not so casual) hints, almost anything in it with sufficient "accord or similarity" is open to a figural interpretation. For example, a passage (cited by Auerbach) from Lactantius's third-century *Divinae institutiones* is tailormade as an account of how a day in the life of Vladimir and Estragon may be seen as a *figura* of human history:

> We have frequently said that small and trivial things are figures and foreshadowings of great things; thus, this day of ours, which is bounded by sunrise and sunset, bears the likeness of that great day which is circumscribed by the passing of a thousand years. In the same way the *figuratio* of man on earth carried with it a parable of the heavenly people yet to be.

Obviously we do not have to resort to figural methodology to reach the conclusion that Vladimir and Estragon stand for "all humanity," and it is equally possible to interpret the play's "day" in a totally secular way: that is, as a *"figuratio"* of man on earth bereft of a God or the remotest possibility of a "heavenly" future. The idea is to show how readily the play's "trivia" will foreshadow "great things" (which are, have been, or will be) if one simply brings them into its vicinity. As a more specific instance of how such "things" inhere in the action, take the little scene in which Vladimir and Estragon "do the tree":

ESTRAGON: The tree?
Vladimir does the tree, staggering about on one leg.
VLADIMIR: (*stopping*) Your turn.
Estragon does the tree, staggers.
ESTRAGON: Do you think God sees me?
VLADIMIR: You must close your eyes.
Estragon closes his eyes, staggers worse
ESTRAGON: (*stopping, brandishing his fists, at the top of his voice*). God have pity on me!
VLADIMIR: (*vexed*). And me?
ESTRAGON: On me! On me! Pity! On me!
Enter Pozzo and Lucky.

Ruby Cohn has suggested that this is a rendition of exercise 52 in the Yoga series, and it is quite possible that Beckett had this in mind. But in terms of the play's Christian symbolism, the scene would be better titled "doing the cross." Here, under the guise of having the characters do exercises "for the balance," the play has them unknowingly act out the episode from which their key scriptural identity derives. It might be argued that this is reading into the play with a vengeance, but if the scene succeeds at all there must be "greater" implications of some sort, since there can be no conceivable interest in two men improving their motor skills late in act 2. And there are at least two "vague similarities" in the shape of this event which authorize the connection with the cross: the first is the very posture that is suggested by "doing" the tree; the other is the direct address to God which recalls the thief's plea to Christ for mercy. (As documented in Luke: "Lord, remember me when thou comest into thy kingdom." The other thief says, "If thou be Christ, save thyself and us.") We can deduce little beyond this (for example, which character is which thief); nor can the identity of the two thieves be strictly equated with Vladimir and Estragon who are simply the play's primary "carriers" of what we might call the two-thieves principle, or the paradox (as Beckett sees it at least) of grace unaccountably given and unaccountably withheld. In fact, the deepest resonances of the Cain/Abel image rest precisely in their being the first *figuratio* of this principle. All this is hopelessly distorted, but if it were made much clearer the scene would not succeed, except perhaps as low comedy, and an actor (or scene designer) would be well advised not to emphasize anything "crosslike" in the proceedings; for one would violate the play to comment openly on what it had taken pains to keep implicit.

In fact, we might view Beckett's whole stylistic problem in *Godot* from just this angle: how to keep this background—which is one term of the play's vast spiritual metaphor—*in* the background, out of the foreground where it would certainly begin dictating terms and reducing the argument of the play to that of an allegory, however dark and perverse, on the order of *Everyman* or *The Castle of Perseverance*. For it is clear: this play cannot afford to exploit its spiritual content too openly (to call God God) or it runs the serious risk of being swamped by heavy ideas, on one hand, or becoming maudlin with concern for man, on the other. To put the question more positively: How (on the theory that form, to some extent, should follow function) can the play maintain an aesthetic distance from its true subject (man after the Fall) which might approximate its audience's spiritual distance from the promise held forth "in the beginning"? Or, as Beckett once put it: How "to find a form which accommodates the mess?"

I think Beckett solved this problem, with the homing instinct of a true eschatologist, by adapting certain qualities of biblical style. The qualities I have in mind are conveniently summarized by Auerbach in *Mimesis:* "certain parts [of the text] brought into high relief, others left obscure, abruptness, suggestive influence of the unexpressed, 'background' quality, multiplicity of meanings and the need for interpretation, universal-historical claims, development of the concept of the historically becoming, and preoccupation with the problematic." Most of these features would probably apply to many modern works which have nothing to do with the Bible or with religious matters; but with respect to mythic "linguistics," as distinct from myth content, the list seems an especially good catalogue of the stylistic features of *Godot*. In other words, *Godot* is not (like MacLeish's *J.B.* or Giraudoux's *Judith*) an old biblical myth in modern dress but a new myth, or story about the plight of modern man, in old dress; it is a parable for today, such as might appear in a latter-day Bible aimed at accommodating modern problems of despair and alienation. Moreover, Beckett has further observed the canons of biblical style in choosing his parable from humble life (two tramps holding the Christian vigil, as opposed to two kings or philosophers); thus, as Auerbach says, he connects the lowest and the highest, *humilitas* and *sublimitas,* so that while speaking simply, as if to children, the text of the play opens "secrets and riddles which are revealed to very few." Again, this may not be unusual in our era of common-man realism, but it helps to account for *Godot*'s unique double appeal: unlike *Endgame* or *Happy Days*—unlike any serious play I can name, in fact—it can be enjoyed as a clown show by children who have no historical or doctrinal memory to interfere with its clowning; and, it goes without saying, critics and theologians are still searching its secrets and riddles with a seemingly endless capacity for Adoration of the Text.

Unfortunately, this description of biblical or "mythic" style suggests that we are dealing with some sort of portable device (like the sonnet form or iambic pentameter) which can be put out on loan. It is not really a style, as such, that I am trying to pin down here but a form of linguistic energy, apparently timeless, which occurs in various degrees of intensity and combination with other forms of energy. When the "charge" is strong enough, it tends to attract the word *mythic,* with or without the approval of anthropology or the dictionary. Like the Sublime, myth is a slippery customer open to all sorts of metaphorical violation; but one is struck by the fact that discussions of myth, or more correctly of the mythic effect, seem to turn eventually on a "background" quality which is not necessarily traceable to an ancestral content originating back in the seasonal mists. Casual usages of the words *myth* and *mythic* imply an arousing of what Yeats called "the emotion of multitude." William Empson says that double plots "work on you like a myth," the idea being that when there are two or more versions of something (the Lear/Gloucester plots, for example), you have the sense of the example disappearing in the precept, or the copy in the archetype. Narrative content is subdued by the rigor of a pattern that appears by fiat of an absent hand and exists, as Alfred N. Whitehead says, in virtue of "the doom of [its] realization. . . . And this doom consigns the pattern to play its part in an uprush of feeling, which is the awakening of infinitude to finite activity."

Pattern of course is not myth; but we cannot go far into myth without encountering the principle of pattern, or repetition-compulsiveness (the serial adventures of an individual myth, the migration of a myth to new contents, etc.). Something like this seems to be behind Levi-Strauss's insistence that a myth consists of all its versions: Freud's version of the Oedipus myth, he says, is just as "authentic" as Sophocles'. So is Seneca's or Voltaire's or Cocteau's. But in any single play or fiction based conspicuously on the Oedipus story, this background quality is likely to be lost, or at least diminished, because the work is simply a new version of what was already (in Sophocles' play) a literary displacement of "the original." It is Oedipus the King who is being imitated, not the intuitive perception which at some lost point in time led to Oedipus. Thus the myth ceases to be a "thinking of the body" and becomes a host for relevant civic discourse. Thebes becomes the scene of a critical cultural issue, just as Argos in Sartre's *The Flies,* becomes the locale in which the problem of Existential freedom is to be examined. Precisely what falls away in these updatings of myth is the background (now in the foreground), the intuitive perception which was expressible only by symbolic concealment, only by calling it what it was not. As such, the literary version of the myth bears the same relation to its "original" content as the psychiatrist's interpretation does to the patient's dream.

In his discussion of the mythical in the Socratic dialogues, Kierkegaard remarks that the age of myth is already past as soon as the question of a mythical representation arises: "As long as the myth is taken for actuality it is not properly myth." My interest here has little to do with what myths actually are, or may be, but with the way a text can behave mythically, or work on us *like* a myth. It seems to me that it does not have only to do with the presence of a myth-content in the text (the Oedipus story, Christ and the thieves, Adam and the Fall, Cain and Abel) but with a particular way in which the text clothes its myth and controls the reader's participation.

On this elusive ground no one is better than Kierkegaard, and since this concept of the mythical is central here I would like to pursue his distinction between myth and the mythical. "It seems superfluous," he says,

> to call attention to the fact that one cannot call [a Platonic dialogue] mythical simply because it contains a reference to some myth, for referring to a myth does not make a representation mythical; nor is it mythical because it uses a myth, for this clearly shows one is above it; nor is a representation mythical because one seeks to transform a myth into an object of belief, for the mythical is not addressed primarily to the understanding but to the imagination. The

mythical requires that the individual abandon himself to
this, and only when the representation oscillates in this
way between the production and reproduction of the
imagination is the representation mythical.

The example Kierkegaard gives is Diotima's narrative of Eros's birth
in the *Symposium*. It is not, however, the allusion to Eros, as a
mythical character, which constitutes the mythical interest in the
dialogue, but the fact that the tale of his parentage—he is the off-
spring of Poros (Plenty) and Penia (Penury)—allows the Idea (the
paradoxical nature of love) to be "seen." In this case, the Idea, which
Socrates has to this point been pursuing dialectically, is that love is a
mean between wisdom and ignorance, fairness and foulness, good
and evil, the divine and the mortal. Through the myth of Eros, this
abstraction is actualized and maintained in the time and space of a
wholly "imaginary reality"; the Idea is "placed outside thought and
entrusted to imagination." The myth is "the Idea in a condition of
estrangement, its externality, . . . its immediate temporality and
spaciality as such."

Many critics would probably find this concept of the mythical
far too fanciful to be of use to the anthropological study of myth. I
cite it here because it illustrates, as well as anything in myth criticism
I have read, the fundamentally creative nature of myth-seeing—that
mystery or "uprush of feeling" that takes place when you suddenly,
or gradually, perceive that the text you are reading is in some devi-
ous or hidden sense "oscillating" (as Kierkegaard says) with something else, being in effect foreordained, though the point of ordination
is nowhere to be seen. It does not have to be a bona fide myth that
is informing the fiction; any recognizable model will serve. For example, the fiction may have generated its own "myth," as Molloy's
Easter journey is iterated by Moran's journey, or more obviously as
act 1 of *Godot* becomes the myth of which act 2 is a new version. This
process of oscillation is perhaps the most compelling sense in which
a reader participates in the creation, or completion, of the Idea a text
is generating (the perception of an object or a person as a symbol is
a narrower version of the same process), and it goes without saying
that it is also the source of a great deal of textual abuse in myth
criticism.

By creative, of course, I do not mean that the reader actually
creates anything; I mean simply that there is a freedom of inference,

passed over to the reader. Half the text, you might say, exists only in him, in his memory; he must "finish" the text on his own, somewhat as children draw a picture in an exercise book by sequentially connecting the numbered dots with straight lines, or as one might "hear" the whole of a familiar song, played at a distance, in intermittent notes that reach the ear.

This may be a metaphoric corruption of the word *mythical*, but it perhaps describes the ground of attraction that certain texts have for readers. One detects and tracks myth in a literary text by undergoing what amounts to a division of mind. As Kierkegaard says, the mythical is not addressed primarily to the understanding but to the imagination. It is "the enthusiasm of the imagination in the service of speculation." Of course, he is speaking here of myth as it works reciprocally with dialectic in the Platonic dialogues, but the same process may occur in nonspeculative experience as well. For example, there is a passage in Beckett's *Proust* that strikes me as being as good an explanation of Kierkegaard's concept of the mythical in Plato as it is of the Proustian remembrance of things past:

> The identification of immediate with past experience, the recurrence of past action or reaction in the present, amounts to a participation between the ideal and the real, imagination and direct apprehension, symbol and substance. Such participation frees the essential reality that is denied to the contemplative as to the active life. What is common to present and past is more essential than either taken separately. Reality, whether approached imaginatively or empirically remains a surface, hermetic. Imagination, applied—a priori—to what is absent, is exercised in vacuo and cannot tolerate the limits of the real. Nor is any direct and purely experimental contact possible between subject and object, because they are automatically separated by the subject's consciousness of perception, and the object loses its purity and becomes a mere intellectual pretext or motive. But, thanks to this reduplication, the experience is at once imaginative and empirical, at once an evocation and direct perception, real without being merely actual, ideal without being merely abstract, the ideal real, the essential, the extratemporal. But if this mystical experience communicates an extratemporal essence, it follows that the communicant is for the moment an extratemporal being.

Although the word Beckett uses here is "mystical," the experience is what one might call the "personal mythical," the sense in which one relives one's own private archetypes.

This is perhaps enough to communicate the sense in which I am using the concept of the mythical. But by way of stretching the implications a step further I would cite one more text that introduces a modern variation of the background principle. I refer to Roland Barthes's *Mythologies,* a book that deals not with the recurrence of old myths but with the manner in which certain phenomena of modern culture (ornamental cookery, guidebooks, plastic, etc.) become mythologized. Myth is conceived by Barthes as a language, or a form, which may attach itself to anything. Myth is speech *"stolen and restored.* Only, speech which is restored is no longer quite that which was stolen: when it was brought back, it was not put exactly in its place. It is this brief act of larceny, this moment taken for a surreptitious faking, which gives mythical speech its benumbed look." One of the central characteristics of myth (to ignore a great deal else in this complex essay) is that it reproduces "the physique of the alibi"; it always has "an elsewhere" at its disposal: "I am not where you think I am: I am where you think I am not."

Godot would not at all qualify as a myth in Barthes's definition (see, for example, his discussion of contemporary poetry as a "regressive" language which "resists myth as much as it can"); the idea I want to recover here is that his "elsewhere" and Auerbach's "background"—secular and religious variations, respectively, of the same principle—seem to me to overlap on substantially the same linguistic goings-on that we find in *Godot.* That is, the play derives a mythic tension from the constant "oscillation" of background and foreground, elsewhere and here, a coming in and out of focus of what are often contradictory loadings of the same shape, much in the manner of that old trick drawing of Jastrow's which is, by turns, a rabbit and a duck. The reading of the play (less so, presumably, seeing it on stage) is thus a constant effort at translation: trivial to profound, comic to serious, temporal to essential, etc., and vice versa. This is not properly an act of translation (except among critics) but an interrupted movement toward, an instability which may be likened to a mild though aesthetically absorbing frustration at the synapse.

This frustration, or creative activity, is continuous in one's reading of the play; it does not well up only in the presence of significant images like Cain and Abel. I can illustrate this on the very lowest verbal level by returning to the image of the cloud in the Cain/Abel passage. If any image in the play carries a near-zero charge it is surely this one. Yet even here, precisely because the image is such a sudden low-pressure "hole" in the excitement, is an instance in which the urge to translate might have trouble escaping its own momentum. What is the cloud doing up there so gratuitously, so ostentatiously "wonderful"? Might it be something more, as Hamlet would have it, a *whale* of a cloud? There is, of course, the good chance that it is simply a cloud, nothing more; but once framed in the attention, possibilities arise; it might, for example, represent nature passing indifferently over "all humanity," like the cloud the wounded Prince Andrey sees going its peaceful pantheistic way over the battlefield at Austerlitz (the situation in progress would certainly support such a reading); or, could it be a cloud with quite a different, and more relevant, kind of god in it, as in those passages in the Bible where God appears in the form of a cloud. The point is not what one can make of the image but that such pockets of emptiness are never reliably insignificant (a word this play flaunts). All this, of course, would scarcely be the case in more realistic fiction where descriptive demands alone guarantee a certain hypertrophy of imagery, purely in the interests of filling out the scene. But in a text so spare, so cunningly random, everything is a lure. Well and good for Beckett to insist there are no symbols where none are intended, but he himself (like a boy who failed to cry wolf) has set the conditions whereby all images, the more off-handed the more suspicious, loom as potential motifs in the grand design.

Beckett and the Problem of Modern Culture

Eric Gans

The most obvious problem of modern culture is that there doesn't seem to be very much more of it. The dearth of "great" writers today is unjustly dismissed as a problem of perspective. For there are scarcely even any *major* writers, those known outside the coteries of specialized amateurs of "nouvelle poésie," "nouveau (nouveau) roman," "nouveau théâtre." There remains, to be sure, at least one eventy-five-year-old writer who constitutes an exception to this generality. But Beckett's greatness lies in his lucidly paradoxical refusal of greatness. To understand Beckett, and above all to understand the problem of modern culture, we must take seriously his description of Bram Van Velde as an exemplary modern artist: "Van Velde . . . is the first to admit that to be an artist is to fail, as no other dare fail, that failure is his world and the shrink from it desertion, art and craft, good housekeeping." That this statement is paradoxical, Beckett freely admits. That failure, as a new criterion of authenticity, becomes a new form of success, that failure to express succeeds in becoming "an expressive act, even if only of itself, of its impossibility, of its obligation," Beckett the Nobel Prize winner is perhaps even more acutely aware today than when, as a little-known postwar novelist, he expressed these paradoxes in his "Three Dialogues" with Georges Duthuit. But paradox is not nonsense, and Beckett's analysis of modern culture may well be the best point of departure we have.

From *Sub-Stance* 11, no. 2 (1982). © 1982 by the Board of Regents of the University of Wisconsin System.

Taken at face value, this analysis very nearly implies the impossibility of art. The "successful" artist is relegated to "arts and crafts," to what we might otherwise call "mass" or "popular" culture. His success is the sign of artistic inauthenticity, of his having set himself a problem that is *a priori* of no esthetic interest precisely because it can be solved. Solving problems was possible, Beckett says or implies elsewhere, for Proust or Joyce; it is no longer possible for artists today. There are no more significant solvable problems left unsolved; success in art is paid for by insignificance, not to say outright plagiarism of earlier solutions. The artist-as-failure, if he is to exist at all, is thus condemned to tread a narrow line between inauthentic success and the truly irremediable failure to produce anything at all. He has nothing to express except his failure to express, which poses a particularly difficult problem, or perhaps I should say "meta-problem" of expression. Yet all this would be of little interest did there not exist artists, and in particular literary artists, whose works constitute worthy solutions of this problem. There are perhaps a few other candidates for this honor; but the most obvious and significant case is no doubt that of Beckett himself, particularly in his theatrical masterpiece *Waiting for Godot*.

If we take Beckett's statements seriously, we should avoid approaching this play in the first place as a success in doing what it does. We must avoid falling into the critical trap of discussing what happens on stage. What happens is precisely what the play succeeds in presenting; but what should interest us is rather what does not happen, what fails to happen, not because the author chooses to make something else happen, but because he fails to make it happen. We should seek in this play, in other words, a two-level structure corresponding to the distinction in Beckett's esthetic between the "problem" that the artist cannot solve, that is, the level on which he "fails to express," and the "meta-problem" that he solves as a result of failing on the first level—the meta-problem, that is, of expressing his failure to express.

That these two levels indeed exist in this play, are in fact structurally evident, is already apparent from its title, particularly in its original French version. *En attendant Godot* is not so much "waiting for Godot" as "*while* waiting for Godot." The "action," such as it is, takes place in an interval of waiting for something else. The primary dramatic action is thus the waiting itself. This primary action may be said to "fail" in a peculiarly Beckettian way. This is not because

Godot never shows up; indeed, his absence is the *sine qua non* of *successful* waiting, since as soon as he arrived the waiting would be over. Vladimir and Estragon are in fact very good at waiting. But this waiting, as the title demonstrates, fails to express itself in the concrete action of the play. To be sure, there is much talk of waiting. But what the characters actually do, even when they talk about waiting, is not waiting but something else. The playwright fails and indeed must fail to portray waiting in this play, because waiting is not action at all, but simple abstract presence on stage. As soon as the characters do anything at all, even if it be standing around in silence—of which they do rather little—it is not waiting itself but what they do *while* waiting, which is to say, the entire action of the play, that successfully expresses Beckett's failure to express waiting. To sum up, then, the very choice of "waiting" as dramatic action condemns the writer to failure, but this is a failure that can be perfectly well expressed in its own right, since everything that happens, or can possibly happen, expresses it.

Both Beckett's "failure" and his "success" in *Waiting for Godot* are of exemplary interest for the understanding not only of "the problem of modern culture," but of culture in general. For not only does his play "succeed" in exemplifying modern culture, it "fails" as an attempt at classical dramaturgy and thus exemplifies, albeit in a negative sense, traditional culture as well. And to the extent that we can imagine the possibility of another play "succeeding" precisely where this one fails, we may derive from Beckett's play a model of successful insignificant, or "popular" culture. In these works, of course, Godot always arrives.

The "failure" of *Godot* as traditional high culture is its only possible means of succeeding. But the precise nature of this failure enlightens us concerning the essence of this culture as well as the present impossibility of pursuing it. For the waiting Beckett proposes as his dramatic subject matter must be understood not as a fortuitously success-proof theme but as a critical comment on the illusions of the cultural enterprise from which he has disassociated himself. Beckett has qualified this enterprise, with especial reference to James Joyce, as that of "mastery." Joyce was a master, he has said; I no longer claim to be one. Now of all activities, dramatic or not, waiting is certainly the least masterful. It is not, to be sure, the characters but the author whose mastery is in question here; neither in tragedy nor in comedy are the protagonists masters of their situation. The difference is that they are its presumed or potential masters. Whether kings or commoners, they seek to dominate their universe, and their failure is the sign of a higher mastery of their world from without, a mastery with which the hidden author is identified. Dramatic characters are the playthings of a fate that only the author can grasp as a whole. The spectators are said to identify with the hero in his tragic or comic fall; but their primary identification is with the author, who, like them, witnesses and judges the hero's actions from offstage. The identification with the hero is what is, in Aristotle's term, "purged"; but this is only possible because the spectators identify not only with the hero but with the author as agent of purgation. It is in Sophocles', not Oedipus's, hands that we place ourselves in our search for esthetic *catharsis*.

Now what characters like Oedipus or Antigone do could scarcely be qualified as "waiting"—they do what they can to resolve their problems, problems which are not merely their own but, in tragedy at least, explicitly those of their society as a whole. Yet because their projects either fail or succeed as the dramatist knew they would, the end result of all their activity is not really very different from that produced by Vladimir and Estragon. No doubt Oedipus contributes to his own demise, but only as an unknowing instrument of fate. The end, for Oedipus as for Beckett's heroes, is really only a matter of time. This the spectator well knows, whose evening in the theater is sandwiched between other worldly activities like eating dinner and undressing for bed. Whatever the nature of the action on stage, its ultimate effect is to take up the time required to bring about a conclusion determined in advance by the dramatist. This end may be staved off or hastened by the actions of the characters, but it is in no way subordinate to them. What Beckett shows by explicitly reducing his characters' primary activity to waiting is that this extra-dramatic conclusion is in effect always of a higher level of necessity than any dramatic activity. The dramatist's apparently superior understanding of the world his heroes attempt to dominate really only reflects an *a priori* structural necessity. For however well or badly motivated his plot, it is he and not the heroes who will have the last word.

But even if the dramatic hero may be said to "await" his fate, surely there is a difference between his awaiting something that will of necessity take place within the world of the play and Beckett's heroes' awaiting a character who never arrives. Precisely. The "fate" of the hero *within* the play is in reality decided *outside* the play by the dramatist. The characters function within a framework the workings of which are outside them—that of the "catharsis" in which spectators and author collaborate. What is being awaited is a process external to the world of the characters. Godot personifies this process. It is worth spending a few minutes on the tiresome question of "whether or not Godot is God" because, like many tiresome questions, it is not so much insignificant as badly posed. Whether Beckett had the English word "God" in mind when he decided to use the French name "Godot" is not a legitimate subject for inquiry. But "God" or not, Godot plays a transcendent role with respect to the scene that is not without clear parallels with sacred phenomena. Godot belongs to the world of the play, but not to that of the stage, and in Beckett's dramaturgy presence on stage possesses a considerably more rigorous significance than in the classical theater. It is Godot's absence that maintains the world of the stage on which the awaiting takes place. Without Godot, our heroes would have nothing to wait for and no place to wait. Their time and place in the stage world are justified by their orientation to this "other-worldly" personage, who can never arrive without violating the condition set in the title of the play—that the action takes place "en attendant." Now this is precisely the role of the sacred in Judeo-Christian society: God never makes himself present, but belief in his presence offstage allows for worldly activity to go on while waiting for his return. And more generally, the role of the sacred in all societies is to guarantee their internal values from without, to constitute the *real* expression of these values that men can only strive to realize imperfectly under the watchful eyes of the gods. In rituals, to be sure, the gods make themselves present; but in secular culture, notably in the theater, the gods generally wait in the wings, appearing at best *ex machina* to conclude the action on stage. This presence is a shadowy one that the characters sometimes attempt to provoke but usually try to put off as long as possible. Beckett's heroes, more humble and more realistic, are content to wait. And by making waiting their central activity, they insure in effect that Godot will never come.

The foregoing remarks suggest some preliminary conclusions concerning the modern culture of artistic "failure" exemplified by this play. The refusal of mastery displays itself in the reduction of the action to a secondary level, in the renouncement of any *dramatic* conflict which would make the world of the stage itself appear—

illusorily, as we have seen—as a place of decision. We identify with only one desire of the characters—that for Godot's arrival, about which they can do nothing, and which, because its object coincides with the end of the play's action, is effectively paradoxical within the context of the play. If traditional drama was, as Aristotle put it, the "imitation of an action," modern drama is the imitation of an inaction that reveals the ultimate insignificance of all dramatic action. Yet our remarks concerning the sacred suggest that, precisely in the demystification of our identification with such action, this play reveals an essential structure of all culture. The "society" formed by Vladimir and Estragon, because its members have no individually dramatic purposes and accomplish no individually dramatic acts, is a qualitatively more universal model of human society than can be provided by the *dramatis personae* of a traditional play. Or to put it more schematically, traditional culture is historical, whereas modern culture is anthropological. Instead of a significant event, *Godot* portrays a period of pure insignificance; but it is precisely for that reason that Beckett's characters form a model of society, that is, an ongoing, essentially stable set of insignificant interactions. Such a model no doubt "fails to express" any significant experience, but it can all the better express the anthropological reality that lies beneath significant experiences. For we may go beyond Beckett's self-irony to point out the positive mastery involved in the failure to express. This "failure" is in fact a transcendence of the subjective desire that imprisons the individual within temporal experience. What must be mastered is not the world but the self; the artist, no longer able to create on the basis of his desire, must eliminate all desire from his creation. And in doing so, he arrives at insight into the fundamental problem of social organization, which is the limitation of the conflicts engendered by desire—the very conflicts that form the subject matter of the traditional theater. Vladimir and Estragon do not become caught up in the illusion that they are participating in significant experiences because they are only acting *en attendant*—but Beckett can only discover this mechanism for avoiding the conflict that arises from "self-expression" because it already exists at the basis of society.

Before elaborating on the social model constituted by the two central figures, which will involve some discussion of the contrasting model formed by Pozzo and Lucky, I would like to clarify the notion of "model" as I use it here, largely in order to dispose of a common critical misunderstanding. To say that Vladimir and Estragon make up an anthropologically valid model of human society is to say that the pair reflects the "human condition"—but it is not at all to say that they "express" it. Our society is like their society, but by no means are "we" like them. Much effort has been expended in attempting to show that these less than distinguished specimens "represent" modern man. But the great interest of Beckett's theater is precisely that his characters' individual reality, whether or not multiplied by two, does not represent anyone—to *represent* being nothing more than an equivalent of to *express*. It is perhaps less urgent today than at the time of the original production at the height of the existentialist era to remind audiences that men are not "essentially" bums whiling away their lives and the play makes no claim that we are. Vladimir and Estragon are like us not negatively, in the futility of their actions, but positively, in that they have solved, at whatever cost, the problem of living in society. What is of universal interest is not the specific content of their interactions, but their general form. Traditional protagonists are models of the individual, to be accepted or rejected; Vladimir and Estragon form *a* model of a minimal human society. To be sure, they are "individuals" with specific traits, but these traits appear to have been chosen in order to make their specificity as unimpressive as possible. We are neither to imitate nor to avoid imitating them; their lackluster status discourages us from ever posing the question.

Let us return to our social model. The first thing we notice is that as "waiters" the two principals virtually never leave the stage, presence on which is made equivalent to waiting. Thus even at the end of each act, when they are presumably to leave the scene for the night, they do not exit until the curtain has fallen. This scenic presence is filled with verbal and gestural pastimes of various sorts, punctuated with exchanges like the following, which occurs five times in the play—twice in the first act and three times in the second: "Estragon—Let's go. Vladimir—We can't. E—Why Not? V—We're waiting for Godot." This sort of dialogue establishes a delicate equilibrium between the pair, who are just different enough from each other not to be mirror images, but not different enough to allow for the development of asymmetric relations of any kind. Vladimir knows Godot, and Estragon doesn't, but Estragon trusts his friend enough to make leaving unthinkable.

Yet the nature of their relation would remain ill defined if it were not contrasted with that of the other inseparable couple, Pozzo and Lucky. It surprises most spectators or readers to learn that this second pair is on stage for over 47 percent of the play and a full 58 percent of the first act (counting pages, not minutes—but the stage time is probably little different). The reason for this surprise is simple; Pozzo and Lucky, however long they stay, are nonparticipants in the action of the play; their appearance is merely something that happens "while waiting." And this despite Pozzo's claim that he is proprietor of the land on which the stage is set. True or not, this claim is founded on the illusion of mastery that makes the Pozzo-Lucky couple a foil to the other. If Vladimir and Estragon form an essentially egalitarian society united in their orientation to other-worldly values, Pozzo and Lucky incarnate—rather pointedly, I think—Hegel's master and slave. Their movement contrasts with the stasis of the first couple and belies the stability of Pozzo's proprietary claim. Within the ahistorical, "anthropological" context established by Vladimir and Estragon, Pozzo and Lucky incarnate a trivialized model of society as history, a model whose very presence in the world of the play is dependent upon the timelessness of this original context.

Pozzo, unlike our friends, waits for no one; his movement across the stage is self-initiated and his sojourn there is only an interlude. He is, however, thankful for this interlude because, like Hegel's master, he needs contact with persons other than his slave, whose status precludes "free" recognition. In this need for outside appreciation, as in its movement on and off the stage, the Pozzo-Lucky society shows itself to be in disequilibrium. As an irruption of the historical onto the "anthropological" stage, it illustrates the place of the traditional culture of mastery within the modern one. This inclusion, which is also a demystification, should be understood in terms not only of conflicting social models but of dramatic esthetics. Vladimir and Estragon are only mildly amusing in themselves; they bore each other, and would soon begin to bore us. Beckett leaves them alone on stage at the beginning for only 15 percent of the play, a little over a fourth of the first act. Pozzo and Lucky, on the other hand, are interesting personages, both for our heroes and for the spectator. The reason for this interest is simple—they "express" the fundamental worldly desire of domination, and both Pozzo's superior airs and Lucky's degradation arouse the "pity and terror" of identification of which the traditional theater was expected to purge us. The episode of Pozzo and Lucky is a "play within a play" of which the two main characters as well as we are spectators. Pozzo's theatricality is an attribute of "historical" society; or to put it another way, the society that he and Lucky incarnate created the theater of mastery as a mirror of itself. Inserted into the broader "anthropological" context of Beckett's play, this theater appears as an inauthentic posturing, a self-contradictory effort to demonstrate to the spectator that it exists independently of his presence. Pozzo and Lucky are worthy of interest because they are curiosities, figures of a contingent social system that traverses the stage because, without knowing it, it needs to be seen there. Beckett's play needs Pozzo and Lucky to provide a center of interest, but this interest is no longer primary, as it was in the traditional theater; it only helps to pass the time. It is anthropological boredom, not historical fascination, that is fundamental.

The theatrical test of these propositions comes in the second act, where Pozzo and Lucky again cross the stage, one blind and the other mute. Pozzo's blindness is a caricature of Oedipus's; he is the master humbled, the victim of hubris. Above all, the temporal degradation of the "historical" pair contrasts with the stability of their opposite numbers, whose existence even shows a few signs of improvement, or at least of random variation—witness the leaves on the once-bare tree, or Estragon's new boots: too loose, whereas the old ones were too tight. The dramatic function of the division of the play into two acts is to mark the different effect of time on the two couples. It is noteworthy that although Vladimir and Estragon recall their previous meeting, Pozzo has lost all memory of the past: the blind, as he says, have no notion of time. Pozzo—in contrast here to the dramatic heroes he caricatures—has no memory of his earlier passage because the world of the stage is no longer a locus of significant experience. His theatrical posturing in the first act must be forgotten because for him it was only an inessential display of an autonomous being that had no real need to display itself. Pozzo has been humbled by fate, but cannot understand the past because his fate has not been determined *in* time but *by* time. His illusion of mastery, in other words, has not been shattered by the ironies of experience, but by the essential disequilibrium of historical existence. Thus although the reappearance of Pozzo and Lucky may have a "cathartic" effect on the audience, it involves no revelation of truth to either one of them. For they are only curiosities to be observed while waiting for Godot.

Thus far we have been preoccupied by the structures of *Waiting for Godot.* But these structures are of interest to us here only because they can be said to reflect those of modern culture in contrast to that of the past. Certainly they reflect those of Beckett's ironic modernism as expounded in the text of "Three Dialogues." But if this is modernism, then we may wonder why only Beckett, that so old-fashioned man of a bygone generation—already forty-seven when *Godot* was first produced in 1953—is practicing it. Beckett's vision of modern culture is anything but a celebration of modernity, which exhibits the most arrogantly determined efforts at mastery of man's material and social, not to say psychological limitations. What Beckett's esthetic denounces in the past is in fact nothing but its "modernity," its faith in historical solutions. Only in a "hyper-modern" era—defined by the possibility of human self-annihilation that seems to be figured in the later plays *Endgame* and *Happy Days*—is a resolutely anti-modern culture possible. But this culture, although it has produced at least one great writer, shows no signs of prospering. True, the renouncement of mastery is not absent from the work of such authors as Robbe-Grillet, Sarraute, Duras, albeit in no case as consistently as in Beckett. But these writers too are today of a past generation that does not appear to have inspired its successor.

The point is not to bewail the end of traditional high culture, but to understand it, and Beckett's work, in its very failure to lead to cultural renewal, is an exemplary source of such understanding. We have thus far taken this author's esthetic of failure as the basis of our analysis, but if we would situate it in a historical vision of culture—if, in a word, we would reject in cultural analysis the admission of necessary failure that Beckett has declared to be the foundation of art—we must explain why this esthetic emerges when it does. Why did the search for mastery of the fictional world, of which Beckett had witnessed and paid homage to such magnificent examples as Proust and Joyce, lead only to a dead end? Why did the search for new mastery come to appear to Beckett as—to again quote from "Three Dialogues"—"doing a little better the same old thing, . . . going a little further along a dreary road"?

The immediate answer to this question is that Proust and Joyce were hard acts to follow. Beckett knew Joyce well enough to realize that his own erudition and word-sense, however considerable, would never permit him to outdo the master at his own game. This is not mere resentment or "anxiety of influence." For the past history of the arts had shown that new creators could always find and explore territories as yet uncharted by their predecessors, however inconquerable they may have been on their own ground. From Balzac to Flaubert to Proust, from Hugo to Baudelaire to Mallarmé, nineteenth-century literature was able to progress to new forms and styles without coming to a standstill, with no writer renouncing the pursuit of new kingdoms to conquer. Why then should Joyce constitute an unconquerable obstacle to further mastery? And why should Beckett's own second-order mastery add to his own discouragement a second-order discouragement for future writers? For Beckett's ploy of non-mastery sacrifices so much that it can doubtless be used only once; failure to be Joyce may produce Beckett, but it is unlikely that failure to be Beckett can lead to any very noteworthy accomplishments.

If we examine the works of such writers as Joyce or Mallarmé, we cannot help but be struck by a nearly desperate extremism. The sonnet in "X" or *Finnegans Wake* is so far from ordinary prose or poetry that one need not be Beckett to wonder whether something still more extreme, even if we assume its creation to be possible, would communicate anything at all to the reader. As Beckett realized, literary mastery, like artistic mastery, had come to the end of its rope. And since this mastery is precisely the supreme value of "culture," we have now come face to face with the central problem of modern culture. Thus far we have examined only its outward appearance; the time has now come to offer some hypotheses concerning its underlying reality.

Up to this point I have made liberal, not to say uncritical use of the notion of "mastery," on the considerable but after all not absolute authority of Beckett. This notion appears first of all to refer to *formal* mastery of instruments, of brushes, paint and words. A little reflection makes it clear that the mastery of form is in effect a mastery of artistic content; for the artist's mastery can only be realized in the "expression" of this content. And this would appear to correspond to Beckett's use of the word. But the very word "culture" suggests a more socially relevant definition of the notion of mastery. Agriculture, from which this originally metaphoric term derives, exemplifies man's domination of nature. The cultivated field is a conquest of humanly useful order from natural "disorder"—the ecological order behind this disorder not being of any immediate relevance to human needs. The metaphorical application of the word "culture" to humans, originally to children and thence to adults, makes the inculcation of familiarity with the great works of art, music, literature and so on the equivalent of a conquest of the natural—and socially inacceptable—"disorder" within man himself. The "cultured" man or woman has presumably conquered his or her natural self by means of a more or less profound acquaintance with "cultural" works. Aristotle's doctrine of *catharsis* is in full keeping with this idea; and its continued pertinence for the arts at least down to the pre-Beckettian era reflects the continuity of the Western cultural enterprise since the Greeks.

The real meaning of artistic "mastery" is thus mastery over human emotions. To accomplish this, the artist must produce convincing representations or "imitations" of situations the experience of which will arouse these emotions; and this in turn requires of him a technical command of his medium. But this chain of "masteries," although real enough, is still too loosely jointed to serve our purpose. In order to pull it tauter, we must examine a bit more closely the disorderly emotions that the cultural work's job is to purge from its spectators. I have already said a few words on this subject *a propos* of Pozzo and Lucky. Our interest in these characters, our identification with them stems, we have observed, from our interest in domination. Our "pity and terror" are aroused because we all desire to be like Pozzo and fear to be like Lucky. The "emotions" purged by culture are, in this case at least, those aroused in us by our common fascination with domination, or as we have been calling it, "mastery." Now let us go one step further from this specific case to a general hypothesis. Literature may be seen to consist of subject matter related to domination or "mastery" and capable of arousing our desire and fear of same. This desire and fear, which, for want of a more precise term, may be identified with the variety of desire that Nietzsche called *ressentiment,* is no doubt a universal human emotion, at least among civilized people. But it changes according to the general experience of "mastery" in different eras, and may thus serve us as the foundation, or what a social scientist would call the "independent variable," of our hypothesis concerning the historical evolution that leads from the beginnings to the end of "culture."

Primitive egalitarian societies, like that of Vladimir and Estragon, do not generate significant *ressentiment* because they involve no significant social differences. This lack of social difference does not mean automatic harmony; on the contrary, it is in such societies that the force of the sacred is greatest. The harmony of these societies is founded on the incarnation of social values in external gods or "ancestors" like Godot.

Secular culture, which is what we generally refer to simply as "culture," first reaches a high level with the Greeks. Greek society was the first to possess some basic traits that are still found in nineteenth-century Europe and that form the social basis for the remarkable continuity of cultural forms—such as, in particular, the drama—over a period of over two and one-half millennia. In the most general terms, and notwithstanding the major differences between the societies of, say, Sophocles' Athens and Racine's Paris, both are characterized by a strong degree of hierarchization limited by certain "countervailing powers" expressed in law and custom, and above all, permitting considerable room for personal initiative in the upper-middle strata. These are the strata that support "culture" and whose *ressentiment* culture both expresses and subjects to the control of *catharsis*.

To say that these "cultural" societies resemble that of Pozzo and Lucky would be a misstatement; it is possible, however, to claim that they could recognize in the representation of Pozzo's pride and downfall a caricature of their cultural forms. Pozzo's superiority to Lucky seems absolute, but Pozzo himself tells us that this was not always the case: Lucky "taught me all these beautiful things. . . . But for him, all my thoughts, all my feelings, would have been of common things." It is precisely the absolute nature of his present superiority, like that of Oedipus "the tyrant," that has brought Pozzo to the near-madness he displays in the first act. Societies based on mastery have cultures based on mastery. The audience's sentiment of, and *ressentiment* of, insuperable social differences makes them accept the artist's mastery of the means of portrayal of these differences, because by submitting to a fictitious, other-worldly portrayal, they are at the same time permitted to identify with the authorial standpoint that transcends and either comically or tragically destroys these differences.

With this admittedly highly simplified vision of traditional society and culture in mind, we may examine how modern society, and consequently modern culture, differ from it. Modern society may or may not deserve the epithet of "classless," but it is certainly characterized by the breakdown of well-defined social hierarchies and by the expansion of the opportunity for social advancement, if not always by the reality of such advancement. There is no doubt that in our society *ressentiment* flourishes more than ever, but because it is constantly being converted into a motive force of worldly action, it can no longer appear justified by the very nature of human society. *Ressentiment* against necessary and insuperable domination—mastery—is one thing; *ressentiment* against the contingent, and often temporary, superiority of others is another. Once individual and collective opportunities exist for reducing and eliminating social inferiority, those who fail can have no recourse to esthetic *catharsis*. At best they may condemn the entire system; but such condemnation, very different from the esthetic transcendence of individual difference that characterizes traditional culture, can lead only to escapist fantasies—or to revolution. Great cultures are precisely those that portray the structures of social reality as inescapable.

The last great literary masters of Western culture, of whom Mallarmé, Proust and Joyce have served us as examples, all recognized, each in his own way, the impending disintegration of traditional social hierarchies and the concomitant degradation of the *ressentiment* that supported traditional culture. Each extended to a radical extreme the traditional artist's mastery of form and content in an attempt to guarantee for his readers the value of their esthetic experience. The author's domination of his world in the face of the most rigorous formal constraint and at the cost of a lifetime of meticulous labor constitutes in each case an ultimate victory over the degraded *ressentiment* inspired by worldly failure. The artist's mastery here becomes very nearly—but never altogether—an end in itself, for it guarantees that at least *this* man's experience is able to express and transcend the feelings inspired by existence in society. In a world where all are part master and part slave, where no one's position is a fixed necessity, the artist becomes in effect the only true master. But he is master over a more and more sparsely populated kingdom; for the *ressentiment* felt by the inhabitants of the real world can receive little or no satisfaction from an art that has learned at great expense to forego all easy satisfactions, that expresses and transcends only the most ultimately necessary emotions—emotions which, at the limit, can no longer be felt by anyone but the artist himself. The last great literary creators were able to stop just short of this limit—although *Finnegans Wake* may well find itself on the other side. Proust's search for lost time takes as its precondition the renouncement of worldly values from within; Proust's reader shares with the narrator a disillusioning experience of social and personal dominance-relations that points to artistic creation as the only *catharsis*. Similarly, Mallarmé's poems demonstrate that the poetic depiction of unsatisfied desire is its only conceivable satisfaction. All these artists, even as they attain the heights of formal mastery, devote themselves to a justification of worldly failure, but it is a failure that corresponds to the highest, most strenuous form of other-worldly success—that of art.

Beckett's esthetic of failure is his answer to the challenge of ever-greater mastery of means and ever-greater refinement of ends. Beckett's "failure" is by no means that of the modern day "man of resentment," nor indeed is that of his characters. Beckett is never a naturalist, even if he has often been so interpreted by "existential" critics. That his characters are bums or inhabitants of garbage cans is in fact the most convincing proof of his refusal of naturalism. Vladimir and Estragon may bewail their fate, but they do not do so as failures in a modern-day competition for status. Their stability reflects their unproblematic acceptance of inferior status. It is in this acceptance that they are the heirs of the clowns of traditional popular culture—a culture that we must be careful to distinguish from that of modern mass entertainment. Yet in traditional society, the clown is merely a foil for the nobler victims of social difference. Vladimir and Estragon are no longer true clowns, even "tragic clowns," for their acceptance of inferiority has become exemplary. It is even, as we have seen, *anthropologically* exemplary, because by submitting humbly and despite anonymous nocturnal beatings to the awaiting of Godot, they reproduce the relatively harmonious and peaceful equilibrium of primitive egalitarian society. In a world where everyone is to some extent a failure, where *ressentiment* can only obtain satisfaction by being continually plowed back into the socioeconomic system, Beckett finds consolation for us in an *absolute* failure, a failure that is founded on the absolute humility of devoting one's time to the inexpressible and irrepresentable nonact of waiting.

Yet neither *Godot* nor Beckett are harbingers of a long-term solution to the problem of modern culture. The nuances of *ressentiment* as expressed in Proust or in Joyce are infinitely subtle; the absence of *ressentiment* has no nuances. The only thing that saves Vladimir and Estragon from boring us is their epilogic relationship to traditional culture. We see this both in their curiosity for Pozzo and Lucky and in their own dialogues. Their clown routines like changing hats and boots are of no great interest in themselves; what interests us in them is that these mere diversions have been dignified by the structural redefinition of all dramatic activity as mere diversion. But this redefinition can only be accomplished once. The esthetics of failure, as opposed to the esthetics of mastery, cannot go on to ever higher successes.

Beckett's Modernity and Medieval Affinities

Edith Kern

Because of a circularity that defies customary logic and linearity, critics have often seen in Samuel Beckett's work an absurdity they believe to be modern and expressive of the world we live in. It is true, of course, that the author has given manifold and striking expression to alogical circularity, so that the unassuming ditty (originally a German children's song) hummed by Didi in *Waiting for Godot* may well be considered emblematic of the author's entire work as it teasingly begins again whenever one expects it to end and, indeed, cannot be brought to any logical ending. In *Molloy* the protagonist's assertion that the first lines of his report were its beginning but are now nearly its end conjures up a similar mood of unending circularity bordering on the absurd. In the year of the celebration of Beckett's seventy-fifth birthday, we might do well, however, to ask whether this mood is exclusively modern and meant to reflect merely the chaos known to us. It would seem to me rather that it is informed by a conception of man that Beckett's works and those of other contemporary authors share with the literature preceding both the rediscovery of Aristotle's *Poetics* and the neoclassical emphasis on rationality and individuality. Not unlike authors of the Middle Ages, Beckett conceives of the individual *sub specie aeternitatis,* and in *Waiting for Godot* this vision is brilliantly dramatized when blind old Pozzo, having fallen over decrepit Lucky, is unable to get up. His cries for help are reluctantly answered by Didi and Gogo, whose

From *Samuel Beckett: Humanistic Perspectives,* edited by Morris Beja, S. E. Gontarski, and Pierre Astier. © 1983 by Ohio State University Press.

efforts end in their own loss of balance, though they reply to Pozzo's inquiry as to who they are: "We are men." Nameless and faceless, mankind is groping to get on its feet, and the same medieval notion of the insignificance of the individual is later epitomized by Pozzo when he proclaims: "One day we were born, one day we shall die, the same day, the same second. . . . They give birth astride of a grave, the light gleams an instant, then it's night once more." Such a conception of man does not call for clearly outlined literary protagonists or psychological explanations. Nor is it concerned with personal confrontations or social problems. The focus is rather on mankind and its unchanging structures and needs within the universe. The individual is but the transitory and ephemeral link in Nature's unending chain of birth, life, and death.

Quite obviously, such a vision of man and the universe affects the function and form of literary dialogue. When it is not employed to develop plot or reveal individual character, dialogue becomes ludic. It is not surprising, therefore, that the verbal exchanges of Beckett's characters often seem absurd to those who approach them with attitudes that conform to neo-classical expectations. But when Didi and Gogo wonder, for instance, whether they should leave, end it all, go on, or come back tomorrow, they engage in conversational patterns of the kind we might encounter in any medieval French farce:

> ESTRAGON: Where shall we go?
> VLADIMIR: Not far.
> ESTRAGON: Oh yes. Let's go far away from here.
> VLADIMIR: We can't.
> ESTRAGON: Why not?
> VLADIMIR: We have to come back tomorrow.
> ESTRAGON: What for?
> VLADIMIR: To wait for Godot.

In his study of French farce, Robert Garapon has referred to such dialogue, which reveals no facts and follows no logical pattern, as "un jeu de paume," and the verbal exchanges of Beckett's characters resemble, indeed, quite frequently verbal ballgames—although the effect may be, on occasion, highly lyrical and poetic. Beckett's own consciousness of this ballgame effect of dialogue is quite apparent. "In the meantime," Gogo suggests on one occasion, "let us try and converse calmly, since we are incapable of keeping silent."

Vladimir—musing why it is that of the four Evangelists "only one speaks of a thief being saved"—prods Estragon, who had remained silent: "Come on, Didi, return the ball." In *Endgame,* of course, Clov's question "What is there to keep me here?" is answered by Hamm with "The dialogue." But in Beckett's work such ludic dialogue may also assume the form of medieval *flyting,* that is, of half-playful, half-serious insults. On one occasion when Didi and Gogo have nothing to do and nowhere to go, as they wait for Godot, they begin to quarrel just to pass the time away. They are close to getting into a fist fight, when Gogo suggests: "That's the idea, let's abuse each other." Stage directions indicate that they turn, move away from each other, and begin to insult each other, one outdoing the other until Didi is utterly vanquished and Gogo calls him "Crritic!" so that Gogo concedes: "Now let's make it up!" In all likelihood, such *flyting* had its origin in more ancient "slanging matches" that, in the view of Johan Huizinga, may well represent the very origin of theater. The exaggerated insults that rival tribes engaged in would have led to violent war, had there not been in existence a tacit understanding that they were meant to be an impersonal game of one-upmanship—a liberation of pent-up emotions in a spirit of make believe, not unlike that of "playing the dozens" known to black communities. It is interesting in this respect that the *iambos,* the meter of Greek tragedy, is thought by some to have meant *derision,* suggesting that theater and the exchange of insults have been linked from time immemorial. In the commedia dell'arte such slanging matches were standard in the lover's pursuit of his beloved and her playful or serious rejection of him. Eugène Ionesco recently used them with great skill in his play *Macbett* (based on Shakespeare's *Macbeth*) to give expression to the snowballing effect of murder, as he has his conspirators reach the tragicomic frenzy of hatred in the course of their verbal exchanges. Beckett availed himself of such tragicomic playfulness mainly in order to be able to discuss questions as serious as those of man's place in the world and his relationship to God, without sounding pompous or transgressing the limits of theater as entertainment and stage business.

In his early works, ludic dialogue and *flyting* permitted Beckett, above all, to juxtapose the sacred and the profane in a mood of the seeming absurdity known to the Middle Ages. Thus Vladimir and Estragon, wondering whether man is *tied* to God (or is it Godot?), have an answer suggested to them that is as ambivalent as it is ironically farcical when Pozzo appears upon the stage led by Lucky, to whom he is tied (or who is tied to him?) by a rope. In *The Absolute Comic*, I have discussed at some length the significance of medieval parodies that, in similar manner, juxtapose the sacred with the profane and whose popularity is attested to by the large number of Latin manuscripts still extant. Their spirit was caught remarkably well by Nietzsche in *Thus Spake Zarathustra*, which contains a travesty of a Mass, not unlike those celebrated during the medieval Festival of the Ass. A brief sampling of it will convey the flavor of such parody in all its carnivalesque irreverence that laughingly turns the world upside down:

> And the litany sounded thus:
> Amen! And glory and honour and wisdom and thanks and praise and strength be to our God, from everlasting to everlasting!
> —The ass, however, here brayed Ye-A.
> He carrieth our burdens, he hath taken upon him the form of a servant, he is patient of heart and never saith Nay; and he who loveth his God chastiseth him.
> —The ass, however, here brayed Ye-A.
> He speaketh not: except that he ever saith Yea to the world which he created: thus doth he extol his world. It is his artfulness that speaketh not: thus is he rarely found wrong.
> —The ass, however, here brayed Ye-A.
> Uncomely goeth he through the world. Grey is the favourite colour in which he wrappeth his virtue. Hath he spirit, then doth he conceal it; every one, however, believeth in his long ears.

Nietzsche's travesty, though used by him in the spirit of satire, would seem to be sacrilegious, unless we recognize that it belongs to that—usually more lighthearted—medieval tradition. It is in this same tradition that James Joyce parodied the litany, the liturgy, and the Lord's Prayer and that his work abounds in ludic travesties such as the following: "Haloed be her eve, her singtime sung, her rill be run, unhemmed as it is uneven." Or: "Oura Vatars that arred in Himmal," with its exuberant fusion of different languages, real as well as invented. Or: "Ouhr Former who erred," a sheer play on sound. Rabelais had indulged in such exuberant and irreverent playfulness in his *Gargantua and Pantagruel,* and in his seminal study *Rabelais and His World,* Mikhail Bakhtin points out that one of the book's protagonists, Panurge, seeking advice from Friar John as to whether he should marry or not, couches his words in praise of the male sexual parts in the form of a litany repeated 153 times. Rabelais used Christ's last words on the cross "sitio" (I thirst) and "consummatum est" (it is finished) in a literal sense as if they referred to food and drink, and such mingling of the sacred and the profane was so readily accepted and enjoyed in the author's time that he did not expunge it from his 1524 edition, which had to pass severe censorship. It would be difficult but also idle to ascertain whether Beckett consciously adopted the spirit of this tradition, or whether it was simply germane to his own concerns. We know, of course, that, like Joyce, he had been a student of Romance literatures and that his early poetry was cast in the Provençal and medieval French forms of the troubadours tradition: the *enueg,* the *planh,* and the *alba.* This "modern minstrel," Harvey wrote, "chooses titles for seven of his thirteen poems directly out of the troubadour tradition." There can be no doubt, at any rate, that in his theater and fiction Beckett perpetuates or reinvents medieval juxtapositions of the sacred and the profane—both in a sense of playfulness and of profound seriousness.

There is, for instance, the narrator of Beckett's *Watt,* identified as Sam somewhere toward the middle of the novel, who conveys to us that, one day, in the garden of his pavilion (it seems to be part of a mental institution), he espied Watt, whom he had previously and intimately known at another place. Watt was walking toward him but was walking backward. As Watt grotesquely advances—perpetually falling into the thorny shrubbery and painfully extricating himself from it—he turns his face toward Sam, who perceives him both as an image of Christ bearing a crown of thorns and as his own mirror image. The identity thus evoked between a religious image of Christ as painted by Bosch and hanging in London's Trafalgar Square, on the one hand, and the half-crazed representative of mankind Watt, who is the grotesque mirror of Sam himself, on the other, would border on the sacrilegious, were we not conscious of the fact that Watt advancing backward and perpetually falling is also a figure of medieval farce, of carnival, and of what I have designated with the Baudelairean term "the absolute comic." Beckett maintains the ambivalence of that absolute comic so that, through laughter and tears, he can seriously probe the meaning of human existence without assuming the part of the philosopher. Beckett's ability and determination to pursue such serious questions under the guise of farce make themselves felt everywhere in his work and prove themselves perhaps most strikingly in a scene of the second novel of his trilogy, *Malone Dies*. There Macmann (Son of Man) is grotesquely caught in the rain, far from shelter, in an open field. Dressed like a scarecrow, he lies down on the ground in the posture of one crucified as the "rain pelted down on his back with the sound . . . of a drum. . . . The idea of punishment came to his mind, addicted, it is true, to that chimera and probably impressed by the posture of the body and the fingers clenched as though in torment. And without knowing exactly what his sin was he felt . . . that living was not a sufficient atonement for it."

But it is above all in Lucky's speech, that torrent of seeming madness, that Beckett's mingling of the sacred and the profane and even the scatological assumes truly medieval aspects. In the manner of participants in medieval farce, Lucky turns traditional patterns of reasoned discourse and theological debate into farce. Yet the seriousness of his concerns becomes apparent when we strip his speech of its carnivalesque elements. He then seems to suggest something like "given the existence . . . of a personal God . . . with white beard . . . outside time . . . who from the heights of divine . . . aphasia loves us dearly with some exceptions for reasons unknown . . . and suffers with those who . . . are plunged in torment . . . it is established beyond all doubt . . . that man . . . fades away." A number of critics more or less agree on such a reading. Yet nothing could better illustrate the half-serious, half-playful travesties of medieval carnival and their ridicule of theological and scholarly pomposity that takes itself too seriously than Lucky's speech. It is clearly patterned after a medieval French *sermon joyeux*, a burlesque sermon of the kind preached in churches during carnivalesque celebrations and that later became part of the threesome that made up French traditional theatrical performances: the *sermon*, the *sottie*, and the *mystère* or *farce*. Rhetorically, the *sermon joyeux* was a *coq-à-l'âne*, a discourse defined as disjointedly passing from one subject to another without logical transition of any sort. "Sauter du coq à l'âne" meant literally "to leap from the rooster to the donkey," and the expression may well have its origin in animal debates. Although the sixteenth-century French poet Marot is credited with the invention of a poetic genre by that name, the concept is clearly much older. In the form of a *coq-à-l'âne*, *sermons joyeux* often travestied sacred texts by speaking of food, drink, and sex as if they were discussing theology or vice versa. The aim of the *sermon joyeux* was, on occasion, satire, but the genre was usually expressive of a sheer joy in verbal fantasy, often starting with Latin invocations, such as "in nomine Patris, et Filii et Spiritus Sancty. Amen." It jumbled together disparate notions and languages and did not hesitate to address itself in the same phrase to Bacchus, Venus, and the Christian God. In its grotesque references and its play on sound rather than meaning, the genre represented a triumph of carnivalesque fantasy, both in exuberance and in irreverence toward all that was taboo. Unfortunately, the examples extant of such *sermons joyeux* are not easily accessible to the modern reader because of their generous mixture of medieval French with an oddly gallicized Latin, so that the genre is, perhaps, most easily illustrated by a sampling from Molière's *Don Juan*. This is how Don Juan is lectured to by his servant Sganarelle:

> I can keep quiet no longer . . . , but I must open my heart to you and tell you that I think as a faithful servant should. You know, master, the pitcher can go to the well once too often, and . . . men in the world are like the bird on the bough, the bough is part of the tree and whoever holds on to the tree is following sound precepts; sound precepts are better than fine words; the court is the place for fine words; at the court you find courtiers, and courtiers do whatever's the fashion. . . . A good pilot needs prudence; young men have no prudence . . . ; old men love riches; riches make men rich; the rich aren't poor; poor men know necessity and necessity knows no law. Without law men live like animals, which all goes to prove that you'll be damned to all eternity.

Lucky's mock sermon abounds, from its start, in scholarly references to authorities that bear names as grotesque and even obscene as Puncher and Wattman, Testew and Cunard, Fartov and Belcher, Peckham Fulham Clapham, Steinweg and Peterman, and Essy-in-Possy. Lucky's elaborate proof of the existence of God is put in question because it is based on the findings of these authorities. Nor do we derive assurance from the childish picture he evokes of a God with white beard, or from the animal-like sounds—quaquaquaqua—with which he accompanies the word God and which in French pronunciation become obscene references to the body and its elimination. A similarly irreverent effect is achieved by Lucky's stutter-

ing proffering of "Acacacacademy" and "Anthropopopometry."
Such phrases as "labors left unfinished," "for reasons unknown,"
together with heaven, hell, flames, and fire conjure up a world pre-
sided over by a god as inscrutable as he is unpredictable, while the
phrase "it is established beyond all doubt" ridicules the foolish and
arrogant certainties of certain scholars. Like a medieval fool, Lucky
truly leaps from topic to topic, as he turns the world mockingly
upside down. But while he engages in *fatrasies,* the farcical play with
words known to the French Middle Ages, he raises serious questions
concerning man and his place in the universe—the same questions, in
fact, that were raised by Didi and Gogo at the beginning of the play,
namely, whether there is a God who loves man dearly and knows
why he saved only one of the two sinners, or whether man's notion
that "time will tell" is as absurd as the certainty of some that knowledge can be "established beyond all doubt." Such questions can be
dealt with, after all, only in the ludic mode of the *coq-à-l'âne.* For
whosoever raises them—be he medieval or modern man—will be
listened to only if he plays the role of the fool.

Seen in this light, the play's title cannot but be recognized as one
of the half-serious, half-playful bilingual combinations so often encountered in medieval French literature—regardless of what immediate experience might have suggested to Beckett the name Godot. It
represents clearly a juxtaposition of the sacred with the profane as it
links the Anglo-Saxon word *God* with the French suffix *-ot* that
abases and makes laughable any name it is attached to, such as
Pierre/Pierrot, Jacques/Jacquot, Charles/Charlot. Such "absurdity"
is not an inadvertent reflection in Beckett's work of the chaotic universe we live in but rather a conscious tool in the hand of an author
who sees man *sub specie aeternitatis,* who ridicules the desire of most
of us, expressed for centuries in literature, to envision himself—not
unlike Hamm in *Endgame*—as the center of the universe, of an author
realizing that he can speak of what is most serious only in the manner
of farce and the absolute comic. I am tempted to impute to Beckett
a passage from Plato quoted by Huizinga: "Though human affairs
are not worthy of great seriousness it is yet necessary to be serious. . . . God alone is worthy of supreme seriousness, but man is
made God's plaything. . . . What then is the right way of living? Life
must be lived as play, playing certain games, making sacrifices, sing-
ing and dancing, and then a man will be able to propitiate the gods,
and defend himself against his enemies, and win in the contest."

Chronology

1906	Born Good Friday, April 13, at Foxrock, near Dublin, second son of William and Mary Beckett, middle class Irish Protestants.
1919–23	Attends Portora Royal School, Enniskillen, a traditional Anglo-Irish boarding school.
1923–27	Attends Trinity College, Dublin; Bachelor of Arts in French and Italian.
1928	Begins two-year fellowship at Ecole Normale Supérieure in Paris. Friendship with Joyce begins, as does immersion in the work of Descartes.
1929	Early writings in *Transition*.
1930	*Whoroscope* wins competition for best poem on the subject of time.
1931	*Proust* published. Returns to Dublin as assistant to Professor of Romance Languages at Trinity. *Le Kid*, parody of Corneille.
1932	Writes unpublished *Dream of Fair to Middling Women*.
1933	Death of William Beckett. Begins three-year stay in London.
1934	*More Pricks than Kicks*.
1936	Travels in Germany. *Echo's Bones*.
1937	Returns to Paris.
1938	Sustains serious stab wound from stranger. Begins relationship with Suzanne Dumesnil. *Murphy*.
1939	Returns to Paris after Irish sojourn.
1940	Is active in French Resistance movement.
1942	Flees to unoccupied France to escape Gestapo. Works as day laborer for two years in farming. Writes *Watt*.
1945	Goes to Ireland after German surrender. Returns to

France for service with Irish Red Cross. Returns to Paris permanently.

1946–50 Productive period of writing in French, including the trilogy *Molloy, Malone meurt,* and *L'Innommable,* and the play *En attendant Godot.*

1947 *Murphy* published in French.

1950 Visits Ireland at the time of his mother's death.

1951 *Molloy* published. *Malone meurt* published.

1952 *Godot* published.

1953 First performance of *Godot* in Paris. *Watt* published. *L'Innommable* published.

1955 *Waiting for Godot* opens in London.

1956 *Waiting for Godot* opens in Miami, Florida, for first American performance.

1957 *All That Fall* broadcast by BBC. *Fin de partie* published; first performance (in French) in London.

1958 *Krapp's Last Tape* and *Endgame* (in English) open in London.

1959 *Embers* broadcast by BBC. Honorary degree from Trinity College, Dublin.

1961 *Comment c'est* published. *Happy Days* opens in New York City. Shares, with Borges, International Publisher's Prize.

1962 Marries Suzanne Dumesnil, March 25. *Words and Music* broadcast by BBC.

1963 *Play* performed at Ulm. *Cascando* broadcast in Paris.

1964 Goes to New York City to help produce his *Film* (with Buster Keaton).

1969 Nobel Prize in literature.

1972 *The Lost Ones.*

1973 *Not I.*

1976 *Ends and Odds; Fizzles; All Strange Away.*

1977 *. . . but the clouds . . .*

1978 *Mirlitonnades* (35 short poems).

1980 *Company; One Evening.*

1981 *Ill Seen Ill Said; Rockaby.*

1983 *Catastrophe.*

Contributors

HAROLD BLOOM, Sterling Professor of the Humanities at Yale University, is author of *The Anxiety of Influence, Poetry and Repression,* and many other volumes of literary criticism. His forthcoming study, *Freud: Transference and Authority,* attempts a full-scale reading of all of Freud's major writings. A MacArthur Prize Fellow, he is the general editor of five series of literary criticism published by Chelsea House.

JOHN FLETCHER is the author of *The Novels of Samuel Beckett, Samuel Beckett's Art,* and *Novel and Reader: Fiction and Its Forms.*

MARTIN ESSLIN is Professor of Drama at Stanford University. He is the author of *Brecht: A Choice of Evils, The Theatre of the Absurd,* and *Pinter, the Playwright.*

RUBY COHN teaches at the University of California at Davis and has written extensively on Samuel Beckett's work.

HUGH KENNER, Professor Emeritus of English at The Johns Hopkins University, is the leading critic of the High Modernists (Pound, Eliot, Joyce) and of Beckett. His books include *The Pound Era* and *The Stoic Comedians.*

RICHARD GILMAN is Professor of Drama at Yale University. His books include *The Confusion of Realms, Common and Uncommon Masks,* and *The Making of Modern Drama.*

BERT O. STATES teaches in the Department of Dramatic Art at the University of California, Santa Barbara.

ERIC GANS is Professor of French at the University of California, Los Angeles. He is the author of *The Discovery of Illusion: Flaubert's*

Early Works, The Origin of Language: A Formal Theory of Representation, and *The End of Culture.*

Edith Kern, who was Professor of Literature at the University of Washington and at the New School for Social Research, has written on Sartre, Molière, and Ionesco. She is the author of *The Absolute Comic* and *Existential Thought and Fictional Technique.*

Bibliography

Alvarez, Alfred. *Beckett.* London: Fontana, 1973.

Baldwin, Helen Louise. *Samuel Beckett's Real Silence.* University Park: Pennsylvania State University Press, 1981.

Bloom, Harold, ed. *Modern Critical Views: Samuel Beckett.* New York: Chelsea House, 1985.

Busi, Frederick. *The Transformation of Godot.* Lexington: University Press of Kentucky, 1980.

Butler, Lance St. John. *Samuel Beckett and the Meaning of Being: A Study in Literature as Philosophy.* London: Macmillan, 1984.

Cohn, Ruby. *Samuel Beckett: The Comic Gamut.* New Brunswick, N.J.: Rutgers University Press, 1962.

————. *Back to Beckett.* Princeton: Princeton University Press, 1973.

————. *Just Play: Beckett's Theatre.* Princeton: Princeton University Press, 1980.

————, ed. *Casebook on* Waiting for Godot. New York: Grove, 1967.

Corfariu, Manuela, and Daniela Roventa-Frumusani. "Absurd Dialogue and Speech Acts: Beckett's *En attendant Godot.*" *Poetics* 13, nos. 1–2 (1984): 119–33.

Cormier, Ramona, and Janis L. Pallister, eds. *Waiting for Death: The Philosophical Significance of Beckett's* En attendant Godot. University: University of Alabama Press, 1979.

Cuddy, Lois A. "Beckett's 'Dead Voices' in *Waiting for Godot:* New Inhabitants of Dante's *Inferno.*" *Modern Language Studies* 12, no. 2 (1982): 48–61.

Duckworth, Colin. *Angel of Darkness: The Dramatic Effect in Samuel Beckett with Special Reference to Eugene Ionesco.* London: Allen & Unwin, 1972.

Esslin, Martin, ed. *Samuel Beckett: A Collection of Critical Essays.* Englewood Cliffs, N.J.: Prentice-Hall, 1965.

Fletcher, John. *Samuel Beckett's Art.* London: Chatto & Windus, 1964.

————. *Beckett, A Study of His Plays.* London: Methuen, 1972.

Hassan, Ihab Habib. *The Literature of Silence, Henry Miller and Samuel Beckett.* New York: Knopf, 1967.

Hassett, Joseph M. "Gödel, Hofstadter, Beckett." *College Literature* 8, no. 3 (1981): 311–12.

Hayman, Ronald. *Samuel Beckett.* New York: Ungar, 1973.

Hesla, David H. *The Shape of Chaos, An Interpretation of the Art of Samuel Beckett.* Minneapolis: University of Minnesota Press, 1971.

Hoffman, Frederic John. *Samuel Beckett: The Language of Self.* Carbondale: Southern Illinois University Press, 1962.

Homan, Sidney. *Beckett's Theaters: Interpretations for Performance.* Lewisburg, Pa.: Bucknell University Press, 1984.

Iser, Wolfgang. "The Art of Failure: The Stifled Laugh in Beckett's Theatre." *Bucknell Review* 26, no. 1 (1981): 139–89.

Journal of Beckett Studies (1974–).

Kenner, Hugh. *A Reader's Guide to Beckett.* New York: Farrar, Straus & Giroux, 1973.

———. *Samuel Beckett, A Critical Study.* Berkeley: University of California Press, 1968.

———. *The Stoic Comedians: Flaubert, Joyce and Beckett.* Berkeley: University of California Press, 1962.

Lyons, Charles R. *Samuel Beckett.* London: Macmillan, 1983.

Nykrog, Per. "In the Ruins of the Past: Reading Beckett Intertextually." *Comparative Literature* 36, no. 4 (1984): 289–311.

O'Brien, William J. "To Hell with Samuel Beckett." In *Foundations of Religious Literacy,* edited by John V. Apczynski, 165–74. Chico, Calif.: Scholars Press, 1983.

Probyn, Clive T. "Waiting for the Word: Samuel Beckett and Wole Soyinka." *Ariel: A Review of International English Literature* 12, no. 3 (1981): 35–48.

Riggs, Larry W. "Slouching toward Consciousness: Destruction of the Spectator-Role in *En attendant Godot* and *Fin de partie.*" *Degré Second: Studies in French Literature* 7 (July 1983): 57–79.

Robinson, Michael. *The Long Sonata of the Dead: A Study of Samuel Beckett.* New York: Grove, 1970.

Rosen, Steven J. *Samuel Beckett and the Pessimistic Tradition.* New Brunswick, N.J.: Rutgers University Press, 1976.

Simpson, Alan. *Beckett and Behan, and a Theatre in Dublin.* London: Routledge & Kegan Paul, 1962.

States, Bert O. *The Shape of Paradox: An Essay on* Waiting for Godot. Berkeley: University of California Press, 1978.

Webb, Eugene. *The Plays of Samuel Beckett.* Seattle: University of Washington Press, 1972.

Acknowledgments

"Bailing Out the Silence" by John Fletcher from *Beckett: A Study of His Plays* by John Fletcher and John Spurling, © 1972, 1978, 1985, 1987 by John Fletcher. Reprinted by permission of the author, Hill & Wang, and Methuen & Co. Ltd.

The Search for the Self" (originally entitled "The Absurdity of the Absurd and the Search for the Self") by Martin Esslin from *The Theatre of the Absurd* by Martin Esslin, © 1961, 1968, 1969 by Martin Esslin. Reprinted by permission of the author, Doubleday Publishing Co., and Methuen & Co. Ltd.

"Waiting" by Ruby Cohn from *Back to Beckett* by Ruby Cohn, © 1973 by Princeton University Press. Reprinted by permission.

"Waiting for Godot" by Hugh Kenner from *A Reader's Guide to Samuel Beckett* by Hugh Kenner, © 1973 by Thames and Hudson Ltd. Reprinted by permission of Farrar, Straus & Giroux, Inc. and Thames and Hudson.

"The Waiting Since" (originally entitled "Beckett") by Richard Gilman from *The Making of Modern Drama* by Richard Gilman, © 1972, 1973, 1974 by Richard Gilman. Reprinted by permission of the author and Farrar, Straus & Giroux, Inc.

"The Language of Myth" by Bert O. States from *The Shape of Paradise: An Essay on Waiting for Godot* by Bert O. States, © 1978 by the Regents of the University of California. Reprinted by permission of the University of California Press.

"Beckett and the Problem of Modern Culture" by Eric Gans from *Sub-stance* 11, no. 2 (1982), © 1982 by the Board of Regents of the University of Wisconsin System. Reprinted by permission.

"Beckett's Modernity and Medieval Affinities" by Edith Kern from *Samuel Beckett: Humanistic Perspectives,* edited by Morris Beja, S. E. Gontarski, and Pierre Astier, © 1983 by the Ohio State University Press. Reprinted by permission. All rights reserved.

Index

Abel, 34, 83–85, 87, 90, 93
Adam, 83, 85, 86, 90
Agamemnon (Aeschylus), 56, 60, 61–62
Albert, Mr., 28. *See also* Vladimir
Aristotle, 98, 106, 111
Attente de Dieu (Weil), 30
Audience, the: as divided from actors, 14; as identified with author, 93–94; role of, 14–15; of San Quentin penitentiary, 23–25; as sharing in waiting, 61
Auerbach, Erich, 86, 88, 89, 93
Augustine, St., 19, 33, 43–44, 79, 80, 86

Bakhtin, Mikhail, 115
Balzac, Honoré de, 30, 70, 105
Barthes, Roland, 82, 93
Baudelaire, Charles-Pierre, 105
Beckett, Samuel: aesthetic of failure of, 95–97, 100, 108–9; and Chekhov, 13; existentialism of, 39–40; on habit as theme, 37–38; on identity of Godot, 7, 26, 70, 74; influences on, 1–6, 112–14; and instructions to actors, 55–56; ironic modernism of, 104; as leader of Theater of the Absurd, 69; on meaning and form, 26; and modern culture, 95–110; motivation for writing *Godot* explained by, 43; on mystical experience, 91; on Proust, 31, 38; and recognition, 6–7; renunciation of mastery by, 97, 104–6; as

representative of Sublime mode, 5–6; skepticism of, 80; on transcendence, 3–4; and two thieves theme, 33–34, 88; on writing in French, 68
Beckett's writings: and the "beyond," 6; criticism of, 67–69; and hopelessness, 4; humor in, 4–5; lack of plot in, 27–28; medieval parallels to, 111–17; "message" in, 21–22, 39–40, 65, 73–74; use of dialogue in, 15–17, 71
Bentley, Eric, 30, 70
Bible, the, 41, 57, 94
Blake, William, 3, 7
Blau, Herbert, 23, 42, 48
Blin, Roger, 12, 42, 44, 45
Bosch, Hieronymus, 115
Bouvard et Pécuchet (Flaubert), 53–54
Boy messenger, the, 11, 34, 37, 78; and conversations with other characters, 12–13, 73; and nonrecognition of Vladimir and Estragon, 32; and symmetry of *Godot*, 20, 43–44, 64–65
Brecht, Bertolt, 42, 69, 76
Büchner, Georg, 69, 77

Cain, 34, 83–85, 87, 90, 93
Camus, Albert, 70
Cassandra, 60, 61
Castle, The (Kafka), 82
Castle of Perseverance, The, 88

127

Paradise Lost (Milton), 2
Pascal, Blaise, 18, 68, 74
"Passion Considered as an Uphill
    Bicycle Race, The" (Jarry), 6
Peer Gynt (Ibsen), 71
Pensées (Pascal), 18, 68
Phenomenology of Mind (Hegel), 41
Pinter, Harold, 16, 25
Pirandello, Luigi, 68
Plato, 7, 92, 118
Poetics (Aristotle), 111
"Power" (Emerson), 4
Pozzo, 11–12, 14, 15; and chance as
    theme, 34–35; as creature of soci-
    ety, 71; downfall of, 9, 31, 98–99,
    102; gestural repetition by, 46; and
    individual's place in universe,
    105–6, 107; as mistaken for
    Godot, 54; monologues of, 9, 17,
    48, 60, 61; and mythical depth of
    dialogue, 78; as performer, 17–18,
    46; and relationship with Lucky,
    15, 19, 29, 42, 47–48, 76, 101–2,
    106; and structure of *Godot*, 20,
    28, 59; and Vladimir and
    Estragon, 16–17, 69
Pozzo and Lucky: and Cain and Abel
    image, 34, 85; contrasted with
    Vladimir and Estragon, 19, 36–37,
    43–44, 102; and domination, 76,
    102, 106; as interlude, 46; symbol-
    ism of, 59, 76, 102; and two
    thieves theme, 45
Prelude, The, 2
Proust, 3, 7, 38, 68, 79, 92
Proust, Marcel, 3, 5, 38; and artistic
    mastery, 96, 104, 105, 108, 109

Rabelais, François, 115
Rilke, Rainer Maria, 3
Robbe-Grillet, Alain, 69, 73, 104
Robinson Crusoe (Defoe), 53

Sam (*Watt*), 115
Sartre. Jean Paul, 39, 90
Schneider, Alan, 26, 42
Schopenhauer, Arthur, 1–2, 3, 7, 9
Seneca, 90
Sermons joyeux, 116–17

Shakespeare, William, 3, 80–81, 83–84,
    113
Shelley, Percy Bysshe, 8–9
Six Characters (Pirandello), 68
Socrates, 91
Sophocles, 89, 90, 99
Strindberg, August, 13, 77
Symposium (Plato), 90–91
Synge, John Millington, 13

Tale of a Tub, A (Swift), 1
Theater of the Absurd, 25–26, 27, 69
"Three Dialogues," 95, 104
Three Sisters, The (Chekhov), 71
Thus Spake Zarathustra (Nietzsche), 114
Time: and change, 31–33; and
    humanity's place in universe, 50,
    65

Ubu (Jarry), 13
Ulysses (Joyce), 1
Unnamable, The, 1, 2, 41

Valentinus, 3, 7
Vladimir, 11–12; anxiety of, 14–15; as
    bum or clown, 17–18, 54–55,
    108–9; and Cain and Abel image,
    83–85; and chance as theme,
    34–35; as character outside society,
    75, 76; and comic misunderstand-
    ings, 16–17; counterintellectualism
    of, 75; dialogue of, 8, 20, 112,
    113; as Didi, 43, 47; on dreaming
    and truth, 65; gestural repetition
    by, 46; as Gnostic, 9; and human
    condition, 37–39, 70–71, 86,
    111–13; metaphysical observations
    of, 50; and need for conversation,
    38–39, 73; as performer, 17–18,
    48; and Pozzo, 58; as prisoner, 72;
    range of emotion of, 46; and
    relationship with Estragon, 13–15,
    19, 29, 71–72; suffering of, 47; and
    suicide theme, 35–36; and time
    and change as themes, 31–33; and
    two thieves theme, 33, 43, 44, 45,
    87–88, 118; and waiting, 47, 96–98
Vladimir and Estragon: contrasted